The Best of
ROBERT
SERVICE

A & C BLACK
London

Reissued 1995
by A&C Black (Publishers) Limited
35 Bedford Row, London WC1R 4JH
ISBN 0-7136-4464-8

This edition first published in Great Britain 1978
by Ernest Benn Limited

A CIP catalogue record of this book
is available from the British Library.

Printed in Great Britain by
Bell and Bain Limited, Glasgow

ROBERT SERVICE
1874 – 1958

Born in Lancashire,
he was educated in Glasgow.
After emigrating to Canada,
he spent eight years in the Yukon,
where he wrote many
of his ballads.
Returning to Europe,
he became a journalist in Paris
and an ambulance driver
in the First World War.
He spent the rest of his
life in France.

CONTENTS

CONTENTS

CONTENTS

THE SPELL OF THE YUKON

I WANTED the gold, and I sought it;
    I scrabbled and mucked like a slave.
Was it famine or scurvy—I fought it;
    I hurled my youth into a grave.
I wanted the gold, and I got it—
    Came out with a fortune last fall,—
Yet somehow life's not what I thought it,
    And somehow the gold isn't all.

No! There's the land. (Have you seen it?)
    It's the cussedest land that I know,
From the big, dizzy mountains that screen it
    To the deep, deathlike valleys below.
Some say God was tired when He made it;
    Some say it's a fine land to shun;
Maybe; but there's some as would trade it
    For no land on earth—and I'm one.

You come to get rich (damned good reason);
    You feel like an exile at first;
You hate it like hell for a season,
    And then you are worse than the worst.
It grips you like some kinds of sinning;
    It twists you from foe to a friend;
It seems it's been since the beginning;
    It seems it will be to the end.

I've stood in some mighty-mouthed hollow
    That's plumb-full of hush to the brim;

THE SPELL OF THE YUKON

I've watched the big, husky sun wallow
  In crimson and gold, and grow dim,
Till the moon set the pearly peaks gleaming,
  And the stars tumbled out, neck and crop;
And I've thought that I surely was dreaming,
  With the peace o' the world piled on top.

The summer—no sweeter was ever;
  The sunshiny woods all athrill;
The grayling aleap in the river,
  The bighorn asleep on the hill.
The strong life that never knows harness;
  The wilds where the caribou call;
The freshness, the freedom, the farness—
  O God! how I'm stuck on it all.

The winter! the brightness that blinds you,
  The white land locked tight as a drum,
The cold fear that follows and finds you,
  The silence that bludgeons you dumb.
The snows that are older than history,
  The woods where the weird shadows slant;
The stillness, the moonlight, the mystery,
  I've bade 'em good-by—but I can't.

There's a land where the mountains are nameless,
  And the rivers all run God knows where;
There are lives that are erring and aimless,
  And deaths that just hang by a hair;
There are hardships that nobody reckons;
  There are valleys unpeopled and still;
There's a land—oh, it beckons and beckons,
  And I want to go back—and I will.

They're making my money diminish;
   I'm sick of the taste of champagne.
Thank God! when I'm skinned to a finish
   I'll pike to the Yukon again.
I'll fight—and you bet it's no sham-fight;
   It's hell!—but I've been there before;
And it's better than this by a damsite—
   So me for the Yukon once more.

There's gold, and it's haunting and haunting;
   It's luring me on as of old;
Yet it isn't the gold that I'm wanting
   So much as just finding the gold.
It's the great, big, broad land 'way up yonder,
   It's the forests where silence has lease;
It's the beauty that thrills me with wonder,
   It's the stillness that fills me with peace.

THE THREE VOICES

THE waves have a story to tell me,
  As I lie on the lonely beach;
Chanting aloft in the pine-tops,
  The wind has a lesson to teach;
But the stars sing an anthem of glory
  I cannot put into speech.

The waves tell of ocean spaces,
  Of hearts that are wild and brave,
Of populous city places,
  Of desolate shores they lave,
Of men who sally in quest of gold
  To sink in an ocean grave.

The wind is a mighty roamer;
  He bids me keep me free,
Clean from the taint of the gold-lust,
  Hardy and pure as he;
Cling with my love to nature,
  As a child to the mother-knee.

But the stars throng out in their glory,
  And they sing of the God in man;
They sing of the Mighty Master,
  Of the loom his fingers span,
Where a star or a soul is a part of the whole,
  And weft in the wondrous plan.

4

Here by the camp-fire's flicker,
   Deep in my blanket curled,
I long for the peace of the pine-gloom,
   When the scroll of the Lord is unfurled,
And the wind and the wave are silent,
   And world is singing to world.

THE LAW OF THE YUKON

Tнıs is the law of the Yukon, and ever she makes it plain:
"Send not your foolish and feeble; send me your strong and
   your sane—
Strong for the red rage of battle; sane, for I harry them sore;
Send me men girt for the combat, men who are grit to the core;
Swift as the panther in triumph, fierce as the bear in defeat,
Sired of a bulldog parent, steeled in the furnace heat.
Send me the best of your breeding, lend me your chosen ones;
Them will I take to my bosom, them will I call my sons;
Them will I gild with my treasure, them will I glut with my
   meat;
But the others—the misfits, the failures—I trample under my
   feet.
Dissolute, damned and despairful, crippled and palsied and
   slain,
Ye would send me the spawn of your gutters— Go! take back
   your spawn again.

"Wild and wide are my borders, stern as death is my sway;
From my ruthless throne I have ruled alone for a million years
   and a day;
Hugging my mighty treasure, waiting for man to come,
Till he swept like a turbid torrent, and after him swept—the
   scum.
The pallid pimp of the dead-line, the enervate of the pen,
One by one I weeded them out, for all that I sought was—
   Men.

One by one I dismayed them, frighting them sore with my
  glooms;
One by one I betrayed them unto my manifold dooms.
Drowned them like rats in my rivers, starved them like curs on
  my plains,
Rotted the flesh that was left them, poisoned the blood in their
  veins;
Burst with my winter upon them, searing forever their sight,
Lashed them with fungus-white faces, whimpering wild in the
  night;

"Staggering blind through the storm-whirl, stumbling mad
  through the snow,
Frozen stiff in the ice-pack, brittle and bent like a bow;
Featureless, formless, forsaken, scented by wolves in their
  flight,
Left for the wind to make music through ribs that are glitter-
  ing white;
Gnawing the black crust of failure, searching the pit of despair,
Crooking the toe in the trigger, trying to patter a prayer;
Going outside with an escort, raving with lips all afoam,
Writing a cheque for a million, driveling feebly of home;
Lost like a louse in the burning . . . or else in the tented town
Seeking a drunkard's solace, sinking and sinking down;
Steeped in the slime at the bottom, dead to a decent world,
Lost 'mid the human flotsam, far on the frontier hurled;
In the camp at the bend of the river, with its dozen saloons
  aglare,
Its gambling dens ariot, its gramophones all ablare;
Crimped with the crimes of a city, sin-ridden and bridled with
  lies,
In the hush of my mountained vastness, in the flush of my mid-
  night skies.

Plague-spots, yet tools of my purpose, so natheless I suffer
    them thrive,
Crushing my Weak in their clutches, that only my Strong may
    survive.

"But the others, the men of my mettle, the men who would
    'stablish my fame
Unto its ultimate issue, winning me honor, not shame;
Searching my uttermost valleys, fighting each step as they go,
Shooting the wrath of my rapids, scaling my ramparts of snow;
Ripping the guts of my mountains, looting the beds of my
    creeks,
Them will I take to my bosom, and speak as a mother speaks.
I am the land that listens, I am the land that broods;
Steeped in eternal beauty, crystalline waters and woods.
Long have I waited lonely, shunned as a thing accurst,
Monstrous, moody, pathetic, the last of the lands and the first;
Visioning camp-fires at twilight, sad with a longing forlorn,
Feeling my womb o'er-pregnant with the seed of cities unborn.
Wild and wide are my borders, stern as death is my sway,
And I wait for the men who will win me—and I will not be won
    in a day;
And I will not be won by weaklings, subtle, suave and mild,
But by men with the hearts of vikings, and the simple faith of a
    child;
Desperate, strong and resistless, unthrottled by fear or defeat,
Them will I gild with my treasure, them will I glut with my
    meat.

"Lofty I stand from each sister land, patient and wearily wise,
With the weight of a world of sadness in my quiet, passionless
    eyes;

Dreaming alone of a people, dreaming alone of a day,
When men shall not rape my riches, and curse me and go away;
Making a bawd of my bounty, fouling the hand that gave—
Till I rise in my wrath and I sweep on their path and I stamp
them into a grave.
Dreaming of men who will bless me, of women esteeming me
good,
Of children born in my borders of radiant motherhood,
Of cities leaping to stature, of fame like a flag unfurled,
As I pour the tide of my riches in the eager lap of the world."

This is the Law of the Yukon, that only the Strong shall thrive;
That surely the Weak shall perish, and only the Fit survive.
Dissolute, damned and despairful, crippled and palsied and slain,
This is the Will of the Yukon,— Lo, how she makes it plain!

THE SONG OF THE WAGE-SLAVE

When the long, long day is over, and the Big Boss gives me my
    pay,
I hope that it won't be hell-fire, as some of the parsons say.
And I hope that it won't be heaven, with some of the parsons
    I've met—
All I want is just quiet, just to rest and forget.
Look at my face, toil-furrowed; look at my calloused hands;
Master, I've done Thy bidding, wrought in Thy many lands—
Wrought for the little masters, big-bellied they be, and rich;
I've done their desire for a daily hire, and I die like a dog in a
    ditch.
I have used the strength Thou hast given, Thou knowest I did
    not shirk;
Threescore years of labor—Thine be the long day's work.
And now, Big Master, I'm broken and bent and twisted and
    scarred,
But I've held my job, and Thou knowest, and Thou will not
    judge me hard.
Thou knowest my sins are many, and often I've played the
    fool—
Whiskey and cards and women, they made me the devil's tool.
I was just like a child with money; I flung it away with a curse,
Feasting a fawning parasite, or glutting a harlot's purse;
Then back to the woods repentant, back to the mill or the mine,
I, the worker of workers, everything in my line.
Everything hard but headwork (I'd no more brains than a kid),
A brute with brute strength to labor, doing as I was bid;
Living in camps with men-folk, a lonely and loveless life;

10

Never knew kiss of sweetheart, never caress of wife.

A brute with brute strength to labor, and they were so far
    above—

Yet I'd gladly have gone to the gallows for one little look of
    Love.

I, with the strength of two men, savage and shy and wild—

Yet how I'd ha' treasured a woman, and the sweet, warm kiss of
    a child!

Well, 'tis Thy world, and Thou knowest. I blaspheme and my
    ways be rude;

But I've lived my life as I found it, and I've done my best to be
    good;

I, the primitive toiler, half naked and grimed to the eyes,

Sweating it deep in their ditches, swining it stark in their sties;

Hurling down forests before me, spanning tumultuous streams;

Down in the ditch building o'er me palaces fairer than dreams;

Boring the rock to the ore-bed, driving the road through the fen,

Resolute, dumb, uncomplaining, a man in a world of men.

Master, I've filled my contract, wrought in Thy many lands;

Not by my sins wilt Thou judge me, but by the work of my
    hands.

Master, I've done Thy bidding, and the light is low in the west,

And the long, long shift is over . . . Master, I've earned it—
    Rest.

THE SHOOTING OF DAN McGREW

A BUNCH of the boys were whooping it up in the Malamute
    saloon;
The kid that handles the music-box was hitting a jag-time tune;
Back of the bar, in a solo game, sat Dangerous Dan McGrew,
And watching his luck was his light-o'-love, the lady that's
    known as Lou.

When out of the night, which was fifty below, and into the din
    and the glare,
There stumbled a miner fresh from the creeks, dog-dirty, and
    loaded for bear.
He looked like a man with a foot in the grave and scarcely the
    strength of a louse,
Yet he tilted a poke of dust on the bar, and he called for drinks
    for the house.
There was none could place the stranger's face, though we
    searched ourselves for a clue;
But we drank his health, and the last to drink was Dangerous
    Dan McGrew.

There's men that somehow just grip your eyes, and hold them
    hard like a spell;
And such was he, and he looked to me like a man who had lived
    in hell;
With a face most hair, and the dreary stare of a dog whose day
    is done,
As he watered the green stuff in his glass, and the drops fell one
    by one.

Then I got to figgering who he was, and wondering what he'd
    do,
And I turned my head—and there watching him was the lady
    that's known as Lou.

His eyes went rubbering round the room, and he seemed in a
    kind of daze,
Till at last that old piano fell in the way of his wandering gaze.
The rag-time kid was having a drink; there was no one else on
    the stool,
So the stranger stumbles across the room, and flops down there
    like a fool.
In a buckskin shirt that was glazed with dirt he sat, and I saw
    him sway;
Then he clutched the keys with his talon hands—my God! but
    that man could play.

Were you ever out in the Great Alone, when the moon was
    awful clear,
And the icy mountains hemmed you in with a silence you most
    could *hear;*
With only the howl of a timber wolf, and you camped there
    in the cold,
A half-dead thing in a stark, dead world, clean mad for the
    muck called gold;
While high overhead, green, yellow and red, the North Lights
    swept in bars?—
Then you've a hunch what the music meant . . . hunger and
    night and the stars.

And hunger not of the belly kind, that's banished with bacon
    and beans,

But the gnawing hunger of lonely men for a home and all that
    it means;
For a fireside far from the cares that are, four walls and a roof
    above;
But oh! so cramful of cosy joy, and crowned with a woman's
    love—
A woman dearer than all the world, and true as Heaven is true—
(God! how ghastly she looks through her rouge,—the lady
    that's known as Lou.)

Then on a sudden the music changed, so soft that you scarce
    could hear;
But you felt that your life had been looted clean of all that it
    once held dear;
That someone had stolen the woman you loved; that her love
    was a devil's lie;
That your guts were gone, and the best for you was to crawl
    away and die.
'Twas the crowning cry of a heart's despair, and it thrilled you
    through and through—
"I guess I'll make it a spread misere," said Dangerous Dan
    McGrew.

The music almost died away . . . then it burst like a pent-up
    flood;
And it seemed to say, "Repay, repay," and my eyes were blind
    with blood.
The thought came back of an ancient wrong, and it stung like a
    frozen lash,
And the lust awoke to kill, to kill . . . then the music stopped
    with a crash,
And the stranger turned, and his eyes they burned in a most
    peculiar way;

In a buckskin shirt that was glazed with dirt he sat, and I saw
him sway;
Then his lips went in in a kind of grin, and he spoke, and his
voice was calm,
And "Boys," says he, "you don't know me, and none of you
care a damn;
But I want to state, and my words are straight, and I'll bet my
poke they're true,
That one of you is a hound of hell . . . and that one is Dan
McGrew."

Then I ducked my head, and the lights went out, and two guns
blazed in the dark,
And a woman screamed, and the lights went up, and two men
lay stiff and stark.
Pitched on his head, and pumped full of lead, was Dangerous
Dan McGrew,
While the man from the creeks lay clutched to the breast of the
lady that's known as Lou.

These are the simple facts of the case, and I guess I ought to
know.
They say that the stranger was crazed with "hooch," and I'm
not denying it's so.
I'm not so wise as the lawyer guys, but strictly between us
two—
The woman that kissed him and—pinched his poke—was the
lady that's known as Lou.

THE CREMATION OF SAM McGEE

There are strange things done in the midnight sun
  By the men who moil for gold;
The Arctic trails have their secret tales
  That would make your blood run cold;
The Northern Lights have seen queer sights,
  But the queerest they ever did see
Was that night on the marge of Lake Lebarge
  I cremated Sam McGee.

Now Sam McGee was from Tennessee, where the cotton blooms and blows.

Why he left his home in the South to roam 'round the Pole, God only knows.

He was always cold, but the land of gold seemed to hold him like a spell;

Though he'd often say in his homely way that "he'd sooner live in hell."

On a Christmas Day we were mushing our way over the Dawson trail.

Talk of your cold! through the parka's fold it stabbed like a driven nail.

If our eyes we'd close, then the lashes froze till sometimes we couldn't see;

It wasn't much fun, but the only one to whimper was Sam McGee.

And that very night, as we lay packed tight in our robes beneath the snow,

And the dogs were fed, and the stars o'erhead were dancing
    heel and toe,
He turned to me, and "Cap," says he, "I'll cash in this trip, I
    guess;
And if I do, I'm asking that you won't refuse my last request."

Well, he seemed so low that I couldn't say no; then he says with
    a sort of moan:
"It's the cursèd cold, and it's got right hold till I'm chilled clean
    through to the bone.
Yet 'tain't being dead—it's my awful dread of the icy grave
    that pains;
So I want you to swear that, foul or fair, you'll cremate my last
    remains."

A pal's last need is a thing to heed, so I swore I would not fail;
And we started on at the streak of dawn; but God! he looked
    ghastly pale.
He crouched on the sleigh, and he raved all day of his home
    in Tennessee;
And before nightfall a corpse was all that was left of Sam
    McGee.

There wasn't a breath in that land of death, and I hurried, horror-
    driven,
With a corpse half hid that I couldn't get rid, because of a
    promise given;
It was lashed to the sleigh, and it seemed to say: "You may tax
    your brawn and brains,
But you promised true, and it's up to you to cremate those last
    remains."

Now a promise made is a debt unpaid, and the trail has its own
    stern code.

In the days to come, though my lips were dumb, in my heart how I cursed that load.

In the long, long night, by the lone firelight, while the huskies, round in a ring,

Howled out their woes to the homeless snows— O God! how I loathed the thing.

And every day that quiet clay seemed to heavy and heavier grow;

And on I went, though the dogs were spent and the grub was getting low;

The trail was bad, and I felt half mad, but I swore I would not give in;

And I'd often sing to the hateful thing, and it hearkened with a grin.

Till I came to the marge of Lake Lebarge, and a derelict there lay;

It was jammed in the ice, but I saw in a trice it was called the "Alice May."

And I looked at it, and I thought a bit, and I looked at my frozen chum;

Then "Here," said I, with a sudden cry, "is my cre-ma-tor-eum."

Some planks I tore from the cabin floor, and I lit the boiler fire;

Some coal I found that was lying around, and I heaped the fuel higher;

The flames just soared, and the furnace roared—such a blaze you seldom see;

And I burrowed a hole in the glowing coal, and I stuffed in Sam McGee.

Then I made a hike, for I didn't like to hear him sizzle so;
And the heavens scowled, and the huskies howled, and the wind
   began to blow.
It was icy cold, but the hot sweat rolled down my cheeks, and I
   don't know why;
And the greasy smoke in an inky cloak went streaking down
   the sky.

I do not know how long in the snow I wrestled with grisly fear;
But the stars came out and they danced about ere again I ven-
   tured near;
I was sick with dread, but I bravely said: "I'll just take a peep
   inside.
I guess he's cooked, and it's time I looked"; . . . then the door
   I opened wide.

And there sat Sam, looking cool and calm, in the heart of the
   furnace roar;
And he wore a smile you could see a mile, and he said: "Please
   close that door.
It's fine in here, but I greatly fear you'll let in the cold and
   storm—
Since I left Plumtree, down in Tennessee, it's the first time I've
   been warm."

> *There are strange things done in the midnight sun*
>   *By the men who moil for gold;*
> *The Arctic trails have their secret tales*
>   *That would make your blood run cold;*
> *The Northern Lights have seen queer sights,*
>   *But the queerest they ever did see*
> *Was that night on the marge of Lake Lebarge*
>   *I cremated Sam McGee.*

MY MADONNA

I HALED me a woman from the street,
    Shameless, but, oh, so fair!
I bade her sit in the model's seat
    And I painted her sitting there.

I hid all trace of her heart unclean;
    I painted a babe at her breast;
I painted her as she might have been
    If the Worst had been the Best.

She laughed at my picture and went away.
    Then came, with a knowing nod,
A connoisseur, and I heard him say;
    " 'Tis Mary, the Mother of God."

So I painted a halo round her hair,
    And I sold her and took my fee,
And she hangs in the church of Saint Hillaire,
    Where you and all may see.

UNFORGOTTEN

I KNOW a garden where the lilies gleam,
    And one who lingers in the sunshine there;
    She is than white-stoled lily far more fair,
And oh, her eyes are heaven-lit with dream!

I know a garret, cold and dark and drear,
    And one who toils and toils with tireless pen,
    Until his brave, sad eyes grow weary—then
He seeks the stars, pale, silent as a seer.

And ah, it's strange; for, desolate and dim,
    Between these two there rolls an ocean wide;
    Yet he is in the garden by her side
And she is in the garret there with him.

THE RECKONING

It's fine to have a blow-out in a fancy restaurant,
With terrapin and canvas-back and all the wine you want;
To enjoy the flowers and music, watch the pretty women pass,
Smoke a choice cigar, and sip the wealthy water in your glass.
It's bully in a high-toned joint to eat and drink your fill,
But it's quite another matter when you
                                        Pay the bill.

It's great to go out every night on fun or pleasure bent;
To wear your glad rags always and to never save a cent;
To drift along regardless, have a good time every trip;
To hit the high spots sometimes, and to let your chances slip;
To know you're acting foolish, yet to go on fooling still,
Till Nature calls a show-down, and you
                                        Pay the bill.

Time has got a little bill—get wise while yet you may,
For the debit side's increasing in a most alarming way;
The things you had no right to do, the things you should have
    done,
They're all put down; it's up to you to pay for every one.
So eat, drink and be merry, have a good time if you will,
But God help you when the time comes, and you
                                        Foot the bill.

THE MEN THAT DON'T FIT IN

THERE's a race of men that don't fit in,
    A race that can't stay still;
So they break the hearts of kith and kin,
    And they roam the world at will.
They range the field and they rove the flood,
    And they climb the mountain's crest;
Theirs is the curse of the gypsy blood,
    And they don't know how to rest.

If they just went straight they might go far;
    They are strong and brave and true;
But they're always tired of the things that are,
    And they want the strange and new.
They say: "Could I find my proper groove,
    What a deep mark I would make!"
So they chop and change, and each fresh move
    Is only a fresh mistake.

And each forgets, as he strips and runs
    With a brilliant, fitful pace,
It's the steady, quiet, plodding ones
    Who win in the lifelong race.
And each forgets that his youth has fled,
    Forgets that his prime is past,
Till he stands one day, with a hope that's dead,
    In the glare of the truth at last.

He has failed, he has failed; he has missed his chance;
    He has just done things by half.

Life's been a jolly good joke on him,
　And now is the time to laugh.
Ha, ha! He is one of the Legion Lost;
　He was never meant to win;
He's a rolling stone, and it's bred in the bone;
　He's a man who won't fit in.

THE LITTLE OLD LOG CABIN

WHEN a man gits on his uppers in a hard-pan sort of town,
  An' he ain't got nothin' comin' an' he can't afford ter eat,
An' he's in a fix for lodgin' an' he wanders up an' down,
  An' you'd fancy he'd been boozin', he's so locoed 'bout the
    feet;
When he's feelin' sneakin' sorry an' his belt is hangin' slack,
  An' his face is peaked an' gray-like an' his heart gits down an'
    whines,
Then he's apt ter git a-thinkin' an' a-wishin' he was back
  In the little ol' log cabin in the shadder of the pines.

When he's on the blazin' desert an' his canteen's sprung a leak,
  An' he's all alone an' crazy an' he's crawlin' like a snail,
An' his tongue's so black an' swollen that it hurts him fer to
    speak,
  An' he gouges down fer water an' the raven's on his trail;
When he's done with care and cursin' an' he feels more like to
    cry,
  An' he sees ol' Death a-grinnin' an' he thinks upon his crimes,
Then he's like ter hev' a vision, as he settles down ter die,
  Of the little ol' log cabin an' the roses an' the vines.

Oh, the little ol' log cabin, it's a solemn shinin' mark,
  When a feller gits ter sinnin' an' a-goin' ter the wall,
An' folks don't understand him an' he's gropin' in the dark,
  An' he's sick of bein' cursed at an' he's longin' fer his call!
When the sun of life's a-sinkin' you can see it 'way above,
  On the hill from out the shadder in a glory 'gin the sky,

An' your mother's voice is callin', an' her arms are stretched in
    love,
  An' somehow you're glad you're goin', an' you ain't a-scared
      to die;
When you'll be like a kid again an' nestle to her breast,
An' never leave its shelter, an' forget, an' love, an' rest.

THE MARCH OF THE DEAD

THE cruel war was over—oh, the triumph was so sweet!
　　We watched the troops returning, through our tears;
There was triumph, triumph, triumph down the scarlet glitter-
　　　　ing street,
　　And you scarce could hear the music for the cheers.
And you scarce could see the house-tops for the flags that flew
　　　　between;
　　The bells were pealing madly to the sky;
And everyone was shouting for the Soldiers of the Queen,
　　And the glory of an age was passing by.

And then there came a shadow, swift and sudden, dark and
　　　　drear;
　　The bells were silent, not an echo stirred.
The flags were drooping sullenly, the men forgot to cheer;
　　We waited, and we never spoke a word.
The sky grew darker, darker, till from out the gloomy rack
　　There came a voice that checked the heart with dread:
"Tear down, tear down your bunting now, and hang up sable
　　　　black;
　　They are coming—it's the Army of the Dead."

They were coming, they were coming, gaunt and ghastly, sad
　　　　and slow;
　　They were coming, all the crimson wrecks of pride;
With faces seared, and cheeks red smeared, and haunting eyes of
　　　　woe,
　　And clotted holes the khaki couldn't hide.

Oh, the clammy brow of anguish! the livid, foam-flecked lips!
　The reeling ranks of ruin swept along!
The limb that trailed, the hand that failed, the bloody finger tips!
　And oh, the dreary rhythm of their song!

"They left us on the veldt-side, but we felt we couldn't stop
　On this, our England's crowning festal day;
We're the men of Magersfontein, we're the men of Spion Kop,
　Colenso—we're the men who had to pay.
We're the men who paid the blood-price. Shall the grave be all
　　our gain?
　You owe us. Long and heavy is the score.
Then cheer us for our glory now, and cheer us for our pain,
　And cheer us as ye never cheered before."

The folks were white and stricken, and each tongue seemed
　　weighted with lead;
　Each heart was clutched in hollow hand of ice;
And every eye was staring at the horror of the dead,
　The pity of the men who paid the price.
They were come, were come to mock us, in the first flush of our
　　peace;
　Through writhing lips their teeth were all agleam;
They were coming in their thousands—oh, would they never
　　cease!
　I closed my eyes, and then—it was a dream.

There was triumph, triumph, triumph down the scarlet gleam-
　　ing street;
　The town was mad; a man was like a boy.
A thousand flags were flaming where the sky and city meet;
　A thousand bells were thundering the joy.

There was music, mirth and sunshine; but some eyes shone with
    regret;
  And while we stun with cheers our homing braves,
O God, in Thy great mercy, let us nevermore forget
  The graves they left behind, the bitter graves.

THE WOMAN AND THE ANGEL

An angel was tired of heaven, as he lounged in the golden street;
His halo was tilted sideways, and his harp lay mute at his feet;
So the Master stooped in His pity, and gave him a pass to go,
For the space of a moon, to the earth-world, to mix with the men
below.

He doffed his celestial garments, scarce waiting to lay them
straight;
He bade good-by to Peter, who stood by the golden gate;
The sexless singers of heaven chanted a fond farewell,
And the imps looked up as they pattered on the red-hot flags
of hell.

Never was seen such an angel—eyes of heavenly blue,
Features that shamed Apollo, hair of a golden hue;
The women simply adored him; his lips were like Cupid's bow;
But he never ventured to use them—and so they voted him slow.

Till at last there came One Woman, a marvel of loveliness,
And she whispered to him: "Do you love me?" And he answered
that woman, "Yes."
And she said: "Put your arms around me, and kiss me, and hold
me—so—"
But fiercely he drew back, saying: "This thing is wrong, and I
know."

Then sweetly she mocked his scruples, and softly she him be-
guiled:
"You, who are verily man among men, speak with the tongue of
a child.

We have outlived the old standards; we have burst, like an over-
tight thong,
The ancient, outworn, Puritanic traditions of Right and
Wrong."

Then the Master feared for His angel, and called him again to
His side,
For oh, the woman was wondrous, and oh, the angel was tried!
And deep in his hell sang the Devil, and this was the strain of his
song:
"The ancient, outworn, Puritanic traditions of Right and
Wrong."

THE HARPY

There was a woman, and she was wise; woefully wise was she;
She was old, so old, yet her years all told were but a score and
three;
And she knew by heart, from finish to start, the Book of In-
iquity.

There is no hope for such as I on earth, nor yet in Heaven;
Unloved I live, unloved I die, unpitied, unforgiven;
A loathèd jade, I ply my trade, unhallowed and unshriven.

I paint my cheeks, for they are white, and cheeks of chalk men
hate;
Mine eyes with wine I make them shine, that man may seek and
sate;
With overhead a lamp of red I sit me down and wait

Until they come, the nightly scum, with drunken eyes aflame;
Your sweethearts, sons, ye scornful ones—'tis I who know their
shame.
The gods, ye see, are brutes to me—and so I play my game.

For life is not the thing we thought, and not the thing we plan;
And Woman in a bitter world must do the best she can—
Must yield the stroke, and bear the yoke, and serve the will of
man;

Must serve his need and ever feed the flame of his desire,
Though be she loved for love alone, or be she loved for hire;
For every man since life began is tainted with the mire.

And though you know he love you so and set you on love's
  throne;
Yet let your eyes but mock his sighs, and let your heart be stone,
Lest you be left (as I was left) attainted and alone.

From love's close kiss to hell's abyss is one sheer flight, I trow,
And wedding ring and bridal bell are will-o'-wisps of woe,
And 'tis not wise to love too well, and this all women know.

Wherefore, the wolf-pack having gorged upon the lamb, their
  prey,
With siren smile and serpent guile I make the wolf-pack pay—
With velvet paws and flensing claws, a tigress roused to slay.

One who in youth sought truest truth and found a devil's lies;
A symbol of the sin of man, a human sacrifice.
Yet shall I blame on man the shame? Could it be otherwise?

Was I not born to walk in scorn where others walk in pride?
The Maker marred, and, evil-starred, I drift upon His tide;
And He alone shall judge His own, so I His judgment bide.

Fate has written a tragedy; its name is "The Human Heart."
The Theatre is the House of Life, Woman the mummer's part;
The Devil enters the prompter's box and the play is ready to
  start.

PREMONITION

'Twas a year ago and the moon was bright
  (Oh, I remember so well, so well);
I walked with my love in a sea of light,
    And the voice of my sweet was a silver bell.
      And sudden the moon grew strangely dull,
        And sudden my love had taken wing;
      I looked on the face of a grinning skull,
        I strained to my heart a ghastly thing.

'Twas but fantasy, for my love lay still
  In my arms, with her tender eyes aglow,
And she wondered why my lips were chill,
    Why I was silent and kissed her so.
      A year has gone and the moon is bright,
        A gibbous moon, like a ghost of woe;
      I sit by a new-made grave to-night,
        And my heart is broken—it's strange, you know.

THE TRAMPS

Can you recall, dear comrade, when we tramped God's land
together,
  And we sang the old, old Earth-song, for our youth was very
  sweet;
When we drank and fought and lusted, as we mocked at tie and
tether,
  Along the road to Anywhere, the wide world at our feet—

Along the road to Anywhere, when each day had its story;
  When time was yet our vassal, and life's jest was still unstale;
When peace unfathomed filled our hearts as, bathed in amber
glory,
  Along the road to Anywhere we watched the sunsets pale?

Alas! the road to Anywhere is pitfalled with disaster;
  There's hunger, want, and weariness, yet O we loved it so!
As on we tramped exultantly, and no man was our master,
  And no man guessed what dreams were ours, as, swinging heel
  and toe,
We tramped the road to Anywhere, the magic road to Any-
where,
The tragic road to Anywhere, such dear, dim years ago.

MEN OF THE HIGH NORTH

Men of the High North, the wild sky is blazing,
  Islands of opal float on silver seas;
Swift splendors kindle, barbaric, amazing;
  Pale ports of amber, golden argosies.
Ringed all around us the proud peaks are glowing;
  Fierce chiefs in council, their wigwam the sky;
Far, far below us the big Yukon flowing,
  Like threaded quicksilver, gleams to the eye.

Men of the High North, you who have known it;
  You in whose hearts its splendors have abode;
Can you renounce it, can you disown it?
  Can you forget it, its glory and its goad?
Where is the hardship, where is the pain of it?
  Lost in the limbo of things you've forgot;
Only remain the guerdon and gain of it;
  Zest of the foray, and God, how you fought!

You who have made good, you foreign faring;
  You money magic to far lands has whirled;
Can you forget those days of vast daring,
  There with your soul on the Top o' the World?
Nights when no peril could keep you awake on
  Spruce boughs you spread for your couch in the snow;
Taste all your feasts like the beans and the bacon
  Fried at the camp-fire at forty below?

Can you remember your huskies all going,
  Barking with joy and their brushes in air;

You in your parka, glad-eyed and glowing,
   Monarch, your subjects the wolf and the bear?
Monarch, your kingdom unravisht and gleaming;
   Mountains your throne, and a river your car;
Crash of a bull moose to rouse you from dreaming;
   Forest your couch, and your candle a star.

You who this faint day the High North is luring
   Unto her vastness, taintlessly sweet;
You who are steel-braced, straight-lipped, enduring,
   Dreadless in danger and dire in defeat:
Honor the High North ever and ever,
   Whether she crown you, or whether she slay;
Suffer her fury, cherish and love her—
   He who would rule he must learn to obey.

Men of the High North, fierce mountains love you,
   Proud rivers leap when you ride on their breast.
See, the austere sky, pensive above you,
   Dons all her jewels to smile on your rest.
Children of Freedom, scornful of frontiers,
   We who are weaklings honor your worth.
Lords of the wilderness, Princes of Pioneers,
   Let's have a rouse that will ring round the earth.

THE BALLAD OF THE BLACK FOX SKIN

I

THERE was Claw-fingered Kitty and Windy Ike living the life
of shame,
When unto them in the Long, Long Night came the man-who-
had-no-name;
Bearing his prize of a black fox pelt, out of the Wild he came.

His cheeks were blanched as the flume-head foam when the
brown spring freshets flow;
Deep in their dark, sin-calcined pits were his sombre eyes aglow;
They knew him far for the fitful man who spat forth blood on
the snow.

"Did ever you see such a skin?" quoth he; "there's nought in the
world so fine—
Such fullness of fur as black as the night, such lustre, such size,
such shine;
It's life to a one-lunged man like me; it's London, it's women,
it's wine.

"The Moose-hides called it the devil-fox, and swore that no man
could kill;
That he who hunted it, soon or late, must surely suffer some ill;
But I laughed at them and their old squaw-tales. Ha! Ha! I'm
laughing still.

"For look ye, the skin—it's as smooth as sin, and black as the
core of the Pit.
By gun or by trap, whatever the hap, I swore I would capture it;
By star and by star afield and afar, I hunted and would not quit.

"For the devil-fox, it was swift and sly, and it seemed to fleer
  at me;
I would wake in fright by the camp-fire light hearing its evil
  glee;
Into my dream its eyes would gleam, and its shadow would I see.

"It sniffed and ran from the ptarmigan I had poisoned to excess;
Unharmed it sped from my wrathful lead ('twas as if I shot by
  guess);
Yet it came by night in the stark moonlight to mock at my
  weariness.

"I tracked it up where the mountains hunch like the vertebrae
  of the world;
I tracked it down to the death-still pits where the avalanche is
  hurled;
From the glooms to the sacerdotal snows, where the carded
  clouds are curled.

"From the vastitudes where the world protrudes through clouds
  like seas up-shoaled,
I held its track till it led me back to the land I had left of old—
The land I had looted many moons. I was weary and sick and
  cold.

"I was sick, soul-sick, of the futile chase, and there and then I
  swore
The foul fiend fox might scathless go, for I would hunt no more;
Then I rubbed mine eyes in a vast surprise—it stood by my
  cabin door.

"A rifle raised in the wraith-like gloom, and a vengeful shot
  that sped;

A howl that would thrill a cream-faced corpse—and the demon
    fox lay dead. . . .
Yet there was never a sign of wound, and never a drop he bled.

"So that was the end of the great black fox, and here is the prize
    I've won;
And now for a drink to cheer me up—I've mushed since the
    early sun;
We'll drink a toast to the sorry ghost of the fox whose race is
    run."

II

Now Claw-fingered Kitty and Windy Ike, bad as the worst
    were they;
In their road-house down by the river-trail they waited and
    watched for prey;
With wine and song they joyed night long, and they slept like
    swine by day.

For things were done in the Midnight Sun that no tongue will
    ever tell;
And men there be who walk earth-free, but whose names are
    writ in hell—
Are writ in flames with the guilty names of Fournier and Labelle.

Put not your trust in a poke of dust would ye sleep the sleep
    of sin;
For there be those who would rob your clothes ere yet the dawn
    comes in;
And a prize likewise in a woman's eyes is a peerless black fox
    skin.

Put your faith in the mountain cat if you lie within his lair;
Trust the fangs of the mother-wolf, and the claws of the lead-
    ripped bear;
But oh, of the wiles and the gold-tooth smiles of a dance-hall
    wench beware!

Wherefore it was beyond all laws that lusts of man restrain,
A man drank deep and sank to sleep never to wake again;
And the Yukon swallowed through a hole the cold corpse of
    the slain.

III

The black fox skin a shadow cast from the roof nigh to the floor;
And sleek it seemed and soft it gleamed, and the woman stroked
    it o'er;
And the man stood by with a brooding eye, and gnashed his
    teeth and swore.

When thieves and thugs fall out and fight there's fell arrears to
    pay;
And soon or late sin meets its fate, and so it fell one day
That Claw-fingered Kitty and Windy Ike fanged up like dogs
    at bay.

"The skin is mine, all mine," she cried; "I did the deed alone."
"It's share and share with a guilt-yoked pair," he hissed in a
    pregnant tone;
And so they snarled like malamutes over a mildewed bone.

And so they fought, by fear untaught, till haply it befell
One dawn of day she slipped away to Dawson town to sell
The fruit of sin, this black fox skin that had made their lives a
    hell.

She slipped away as still he lay, she clutched the wondrous fur;
Her pulses beat, her foot was fleet, her fear was as a spur;
She laughed with glee, she did not see him rise and follow her.

The bluffs uprear and grimly peer far over Dawson town;
They see its lights a blaze o' nights and harshly they look down;
They mock the plan and plot of man with grim, ironic frown.

The trail was steep; 'twas at the time when swiftly sinks the
    snow;
All honey-combed, the river ice was rotting down below;
The river chafed beneath its rind with many a mighty throe.

And up the swift and oozy drift a woman climbed in fear,
Clutching to her a black fox fur as if she held it dear;
And hard she pressed it to her breast—then Windy Ike drew
    near.

She made no moan—her heart was stone—she read his smiling
    face,
And like a dream flashed all her life's dark horror and disgrace;
A moment only—with a snarl he hurled her into space.

She rolled for nigh an hundred feet; she bounded like a ball;
From crag to crag she caromed down through snow and timber
    fall; . . .
A hole gaped in the river ice; the spray flashed—that was all.

A bird sang for the joy of spring, so piercing sweet and frail;
And blinding bright the land was dight in gay and glittering
    mail;
And with a wondrous black fox skin a man slid down the trail.

IV

A wedge-faced man there was who ran along the river bank,
Who stumbled through each drift and slough, and ever slipped
    and sank,
And ever cursed his Maker's name, and ever "hooch" he drank.

He travelled like a hunted thing, hard harried, sore distrest;
The old grandmother moon crept out from her cloud-quilted
    nest;
The aged mountains mocked at him in their primeval rest.

Grim shadows diapered the snow; the air was strangely mild;
The valley's girth was dumb with mirth, the laughter of the
    wild;
The still sardonic laughter of an ogre o'er a child.

The river writhed beneath the ice; it groaned like one in pain,
And yawning chasms opened wide, and closed and yawned
    again;
And sheets of silver heaved on high until they split in twain.

From out the road-house by the trail they saw a man afar
Make for the narrow river-reach where the swift cross-currents
    are;
Where, frail and worn, the ice is torn and the angry waters jar.

But they did not see him crash and sink into the icy flow;
They did not see him clinging there, gripped by the undertow,
Clawing with bleeding finger-nails at the jagged ice and snow.

They found a note beside the hole where he had stumbled in:
"Here met his fate by evil luck a man who lived in sin,
And to the one who loves me least I leave this black fox skin."

And strange it is; for, though they searched the river all around,
No trace or sign of black fox skin was ever after found;
Though one man said he saw the tread of *hoofs* deep in the
   ground.

THE BALLAD OF BLASPHEMOUS BILL

I took a contract to bury the body of blasphemous Bill MacKie,
Whenever, wherever or whatsoever the manner of death he
    die—
Whether he die in the light o' day or under the peak-faced
    moon;
In cabin or dance-hall, camp or dive, mucklucks or patent shoon;
On velvet tundra or virgin peak, by glacier, drift or draw;
In muskeg hollow or canyon gloom, by avalanche, fang or claw;
By battle, murder or sudden wealth, by pestilence, hooch or
    lead—
I swore on the Book I would follow and look till I found my
    tombless dead.

For Bill was a dainty kind of cuss, and his mind was mighty sot
On a dinky patch with flowers and grass in a civilized bone-
    yard lot.
And where he died or how he died, it didn't matter a damn
So long as he had a grave with frills and a tombstone "epigram."
So I promised him, and he paid the price in good cheechako coin
(Which the same I blowed in that very night down in the
    Tenderloin).
Then I painted a three-foot slab of pine: "Here lies poor Bill
    MacKie,"
And I hung it up on my cabin wall and I waited for Bill to die.

Years passed away, and at last one day came a squaw with a
    story strange,
Of a long-deserted line of traps 'way back of the Bighorn range,

Of a little hut by the great divide, and a white man stiff and still,
Lying there by his lonesome self, and I figured it must be Bill.
So I thought of the contract I'd made with him, and I took down
    from the shelf
The swell black box with the silver plate he'd picked out for
    hisself;
And I packed it full of grub and "hooch," and I slung it on the
    sleigh;
Then I harnessed up my team of dogs and was off at dawn of day.

You know what it's like in the Yukon wild when it's sixty-nine
    below;
When the ice-worms wriggle their purple heads through the
    crust of the pale blue snow;
When the pine-trees crack like little guns in the silence of the
    wood,
And the icicles hang down like tusks under the parka hood;
When the stove-pipe smoke breaks sudden off, and the sky is
    weirdly lit,
And the careless feel of a bit of steel burns like a red-hot spit;
When the mercury is a frozen ball, and the frost-fiend stalks to
    kill—
Well, it was just like that that day when I set out to look for Bill.

Oh, the awful hush that seemed to crush me down on every
    hand,
As I blundered blind with a trail to find through that blank and
    bitter land;
Half dazed, half crazed in the winter wild, with its grim heart-
    breaking woes,
And the ruthless strife for a grip on life that only the sourdough
    knows!
North by the compass, North I pressed; river and peak and plain

Passed like a dream I slept to lose and I waked to dream again.

River and plain and mighty peak—and who could stand un-
awed?
As their summits blazed, he could stand undazed at the foot of
the throne of God.
North, aye, North, through a land accurst, shunned by the
scouring brutes,
And all I heard was my own harsh word and the whine of the
malamutes,
Till at last I came to a cabin squat, built in the side of a hill,
And I burst in the door, and there on the floor, frozen to death,
lay Bill.

Ice, white ice, like a winding-sheet, sheathing each smoke-
grimed wall;
Ice on the stove-pipe, ice on the bed, ice gleaming over all;
Sparkling ice on the dead man's chest, glittering ice in his hair,
Ice on his fingers, ice in his heart, ice in his glassy stare;
Hard as a log and trussed like a frog, with his arms and legs
outspread.
I gazed at the coffin I'd brought for him, and I gazed at the
gruesome dead,
And at last I spoke: "Bill liked his joke; but still, goldarn his eyes,
A man had ought to consider his mates in the way he goes and
dies."

Have you ever stood in an Arctic hut in the shadow of the Pole,
With a little coffin six by three and a grief you can't control?
Have you ever sat by a frozen corpse that looks at you with a
grin,
And that seems to say: "You may try all day, but you'll never
jam me in"?

I'm not a man of the quitting kind, but I never felt so blue
As I sat there gazing at that stiff and studying what I'd do.
Then I rose and I kicked off the husky dogs that were nosing
round about,
And I lit a roaring fire in the stove, and I started to thaw Bill out.

Well, I thawed and thawed for thirteen days, but it didn't seem
no good;
His arms and legs stuck out like pegs, as if they was made of
wood.
Till at last I said: "It ain't no use—he's froze too hard to thaw;
He's obstinate, and he won't lie straight, so I guess I got to—
saw."
So I sawed off poor Bill's arms and legs, and I laid him snug and
straight
In the little coffin he picked hisself, with the dinky silver plate,
And I came nigh near to shedding a tear as I nailed him safely
down;
Then I stowed him away in my Yukon sleigh, and I started back
to town.

So I buried him as the contract was in a narrow grave and deep,
And there he's waiting the Great Clean-up, when the Judgment
sluice-heads sweep;
And I smoke my pipe and I meditate in the light of the Midnight
Sun,
And sometimes I wonder if they *was*, the awful things I done.
And as I sit and the parson talks, expounding of the Law,
I often think of poor old Bill—*and how hard he was to saw.*

THE BALLAD OF ONE-EYED MIKE

*This is the tale that was told to me by the man with the crystal
eye,*
*As I smoked my pipe in the camp-fire light, and the Glories
swept the sky;*
*As the Northlights gleamed and curved and streamed, and the
bottle of "hooch" was dry.*

A man once aimed that my life be shamed, and wrought me a
deathly wrong;
I vowed one day I would well repay, but the heft of his hate
was strong.
He thonged me East and he thonged me West; he harried me
back and forth,
Till I fled in fright from his peerless spite to the bleak, bald-
headed North.

And there I lay, and for many a day I hatched plan after plan,
For a golden haul of the wherewithal to crush and to kill my
man;
And there I strove, and there I clove through the drift of icy
streams;
And there I fought, and there I sought for the pay-streak of my
dreams.

So twenty years, with their hopes and fears and smiles and tears
and such,
Went by and left me long bereft of hope of the Midas touch;
About as fat as a chancel rat, and lo! despite my will,

49

In the weary fight I had clean lost sight of the man I sought to
    kill.

'Twas so far away, that evil day when I prayed the Prince of
    Gloom
For the savage strength and the sullen length of life to work his
    doom.
Nor sign nor word had I seen or heard, and it happed so long
    ago;
My youth was gone and my memory wan, and I willed it even so.

It fell one night in the waning light by the Yukon's oily flow,
I smoked and sat as I marvelled at the sky's port-winey glow;
Till it paled away to an absinthe gray, and the river seemed to
    shrink,
All wobbly flakes and wriggling snakes and goblin eyes a-wink.

'Twas weird to see and it 'wildered me in a queer, hypnotic
    dream,
Till I saw a spot like an inky blot come floating down the stream;
It bobbed and swung; it sheered and hung; it romped round in
    a ring;
It seemed to play in a tricksome way; it sure was a merry thing.

In freakish flights strange oily lights came fluttering round its
    head,
Like butterflies of a monster size—then I knew it for the Dead.
Its face was rubbed and slicked and scrubbed as smooth as a
    shaven pate;
In the silver snakes that the water makes it gleamed like a dinner-
    plate.

It gurgled near, and clear and clear and large and large it grew;
It stood upright in a ring of light and it looked me through and
    through.
It weltered round with a woozy sound, and ere I could retreat,
With the witless roll of a sodden soul it wantoned to my feet.

And here I swear by this Cross I wear, I heard that "floater" say:
"I am the man from whom you ran, the man you sought to slay.
That you may note and gaze and gloat, and say 'Revenge is
    sweet,'
In the grit and grime of the river's slime I am rotting at your feet.

"The ill we rue we must e'en undo, though it rive us bone from
    bone;
So it came about that I sought you out, for I prayed I might
    atone.
I did you wrong, and for long and long I sought where you
    might live;
And now you're found, though I'm dead and drowned, I beg
    you to forgive."

So sad it seemed, and its cheek-bones gleamed, and its fingers
    flicked the shore;
And it lapped and lay in a weary way, and its hands met to
    implore;
That I gently said: "Poor, restless dead, I would never work you
    woe;
Though the wrong you rue you can ne'er undo, I forgave you
    long ago."

Then, wonder-wise, I rubbed my eyes and I woke from a horrid
    dream.

The moon rode high in the naked sky, and something bobbed
in the stream.
It held my sight in a patch of light, and then it sheered from the
shore;
It dipped and sank by a hollow bank, and I never saw it more.

This was the tale he told to me, that man so warped and gray,
Ere he slept and dreamed, and the camp-fire gleamed in his eye
in a wolfish way—
That crystal eye that raked the sky in the weird Auroral ray.

MY FRIENDS

THE man above was a murderer, the man below was a thief,
And I lay there in the bunk between, ailing beyond belief,
A weary armful of skin and bone, wasted with pain and grief.

My feet were froze, and the lifeless toes were purple and green
and gray;
The little flesh that clung to my bones, you could punch it in
holes like clay;
The skin on my gums was a sullen black, and slowly peeling
away.

I was sure enough in a direful fix, and often I wondered why
They did not take the chance that was left and leave me alone
to die,
Or finish me off with a dose of dope—so utterly lost was I.

But no; they brewed me the green-spruce tea, and nursed me
there like a child;
And the homicide he was good to me, and bathed my sores and
smiled;
And the thief he starved that I might be fed, and his eyes were
kind and mild.

Yet they were woefully wicked men, and often at night in pain
I heard the murderer speak of his deed and dream it over again;
I heard the poor thief sorrowing for the dead self he had slain.

I'll never forget that bitter dawn, so evil, askew and gray,
When they wrapped me round in the skins of beasts and they
bore me to a sleigh,
And we started out with the nearest post an hundred miles away.

I'll never forget the trail they broke, with its tense, unuttered
woe;
And the crunch, crunch, crunch as their snowshoes sank through
the crust of the hollow snow;
And my breath would fai!, and every beat of my heart was like
a blow.

And oftentimes I would die the death, yet wake up to life anew;
The sun would be all ablaze on the waste, and the sky a blighting
blue,
And the tears would rise in my snow-blind eyes and furrow my
cheeks like dew.

And the camps we made when their strength outplayed and the
day was pinched and wan;
And oh, the joy of that blessed halt, and how I did dread the
dawn;
And how I hated the weary men who rose and dragged me on.

And oh, how I begged to rest, to rest—the snow was so sweet a
shroud;
And oh, how I cried when they urged me on, cried and cursed
them aloud;
Yet on they strained, all racked and pained, and sorely their
backs were bowed.

And then it was all like a lurid dream, and I prayed for a swift
release

From the ruthless ones who would not leave me to die alone
    in peace;
Till I wakened up and I found myself at the post of the Mounted
    Police.

And there was my friend the murderer, and there was my friend
    the thief,
With bracelets of steel around their wrists, and wicked beyond
    belief:
But when they come to God's judgment seat—may I be allowed
    the brief.

THE PROSPECTOR

I STROLLED up old Bonanza, where I staked in ninety-eight,
    A-purpose to revisit the old claim.
I kept thinking mighty sadly of the funny ways of Fate,
    And the lads who once were with me in the game.
Poor boys, they're down-and-outers, and there's scarcely one
      to-day
    Can show a dozen colors in his poke;
And me, I'm still prospecting, old and battered, gaunt and gray,
    And I'm looking for a grub-stake, and I'm broke.

I strolled up old Bonanza. The same old moon looked down;
    The same old landmarks seemed to yearn to me;
But the cabins all were silent, and the flat, once like a town,
    Was mighty still and lonesome-like to see.
There were piles and piles of tailings where we toiled with pick
      and pan,
    And turning round a bend I heard a roar,
And there a giant gold-ship of the very newest plan
    Was tearing chunks of pay-dirt from the shore.

It wallowed in its water-bed; it burrowed, heaved and swung;
    It gnawed its way ahead with grunts and sighs;
Its bill of fare was rock and sand; the tailings were its dung;
    It glared around with fierce electric eyes.
Full fifty buckets crammed its maw; it bellowed out for more;
    It looked like some great monster in the gloom.
With two to feed its sateless greed, it worked for seven score,
    And I sighed: "Ah, old-time miner, here's your doom!"

The idle windlass turns to rust; the sagging sluice-box falls;
  The holes you digged are water to the brim;
Your little sod-roofed cabins with the snugly moss-chinked
    walls
  Are deathly now and mouldering and dim.
The battle-field is silent where of old you fought it out;
  The claims you fiercely won are lost and sold.
But there's a little army that they'll never put to rout—
  The men who simply live to seek the gold.

The men who can't remember when they learned to swing a
    pack,
  Or in what lawless land the quest began;
The solitary seeker with his grub-stake on his back,
  The restless buccaneer of pick and pan.
On the mesas of the Southland, on the tundras of the North,
  You will find us, changed in face but still the same;
And it isn't need, it isn't greed that sends us faring forth—
  It's the fever, it's the glory of the game.

For once you've panned the speckled sand and seen the bonny
    dust,
  Its peerless brightness blinds you like a spell;
It's little else you care about; you go because you must,
  And you feel that you could follow it to hell.
You'd follow it in hunger, and you'd follow it in cold;
  You'd follow it in solitude and pain;
And when you're stiff and battened down let someone whisper
    "Gold,"
  You're lief to rise and follow it again.

Yet look you, if I find the stuff it's just like so much dirt;
  I fling it to the four winds like a child.

It's wine and painted women and the things that do me hurt,
  Till I crawl back, beggared, broken, to the Wild.
Till I crawl back, sapped and sodden, to my grub-stake and my
      tent—
  There's a city, there's an army (hear them shout).
There's the gold in millions, millions, but I haven't got a cent;
  And oh, it's me, it's me that found it out.

It was my dream that made it good, my dream that made me go
  To lands of dread and death disprized of man;
But oh, I've known a glory that their hearts will never know,
  When I picked the first big nugget from my pan.
It's still my dream, my dauntless dream, that drives me forth
      once more
  To seek and starve and suffer in the Vast;
That heaps my heart with eager hope, that glimmers on before—
  My dream that will uplift me to the last.

Perhaps I am stark crazy, but there's none of you too sane;
  It's just a little matter of degree.
My hobby is to hunt out gold; it's fortressed in my brain;
  It's life and love and wife and home to me.
And I'll strike it, yes, I'll strike it; I've a hunch I cannot fail;
  I've a vision, I've a prompting, I've a call;
I hear the hoarse stampeding of an army on my trail,
  To the last, the greatest gold camp of them all.

Beyond the shark-tooth ranges sawing savage at the sky
  There's a lowering land no white man ever struck;
There's gold, there's gold in millions, and I'll find it if I die.
  And I'm going there once more to try my luck.
Maybe I'll fail—what matter? It's a mandate, it's a vow;
  And when in lands of dreariness and dread

You seek the last lone frontier, far beyond your frontiers now,
  You will find the old prospector, silent, dead.

You will find a tattered tent-pole with a ragged robe below it;
  You will find a rusted gold-pan on the sod;
You will find the claim I'm seeking, with my bones as stakes to
      show it;
  But I've sought the last Recorder, and He's—God.

THE SONG OF THE MOUTH-ORGAN

(With apologies to the singer of the "Song of the Banjo.")

I'm a homely little bit of tin and bone;
    I'm beloved by the Legion of the Lost;
I haven't got a "vox humana" tone,
    And a dime or two will satisfy my cost.
I don't attempt your high-falutin' flights;
    I am more or less uncertain on the key;
But I tell you, boys, there's lots and lots of nights
    When you've taken mighty comfort out of me.

I weigh an ounce or two, and I'm so small
    You can pack me in the pocket of your vest;
And when at night so wearily you crawl
    Into your bunk and stretch your limbs to rest,
You take me out and play me soft and low,
    The simple songs that trouble your heartstrings:
The tunes you used to fancy long ago,
    Before you made a rotten mess of things.

Then a dreamy look will come into your eyes,
    And you break off in the middle of a note;
And then, with just the dreariest of sighs,
    You drop me in the pocket of your coat.
But somehow I have bucked you up a bit;
    And, as you turn around and face the wall,
You don't feel quite so spineless and unfit—
    You're not so bad a fellow after all.

60

Do you recollect the bitter Arctic night;
  Your camp beside the canyon on the trail;
Your tent a tiny square of orange light;
  The moon above consumptive-like and pale;
Your supper cooked, your little stove aglow;
  You tired, but snug and happy as a child?
Then 'twas "Turkey in the Straw" till your lips were nearly
      raw,
  And you hurled your bold defiance at the Wild.

Do you recollect the flashing, lashing pain;
  The gulf of humid blackness overhead;
The lightning making rapiers of the rain;
  The cattle-horns like candles of the dead;
You sitting on your bronco there alone,
  In your slicker, saddle-sore and sick with cold?
Do you think the silent herd did not hear "The Mocking Bird,"
  Or relish "Silver Threads among the Gold"?

Do you recollect the wild Magellan coast;
  The head-winds and the icy, roaring seas;
The nights you thought that everything was lost;
  The days you toiled in water to your knees;
The frozen ratlines shrieking in the gale;
  The hissing steeps and gulfs of livid foam:
When you cheered your messmates nine with "Ben Bolt" and
      "Clementine,"
  And "Dixie Land" and "Seeing Nellie Home"?

Let the jammy banjo voice the Younger Son,
  Who waits for his remittance to arrive;
I represent the grimy, gritty one,
  Who sweats his bones to keep himself alive;

Who's up against the real thing from his birth;
  Whose heritage is hard and bitter toil;
I voice the weary, smeary ones of earth,
  The helots of the sea and of the soil.

I'm the Steinway of strange mischief and mischance;
  I'm the Stradivarius of blank defeat;
In the down-world, when the devil leads the dance,
  I am simply and symbolically meet;
I'm the irrepressive spirit of mankind;
  I'm the small boy playing knuckle down with Death;
At the end of all things known, where God's rubbish-heap is
    thrown,
  I shrill impudent triumph at a breath.

I'm a humble little bit of tin and horn;
  I'm a byword, I'm a plaything, I'm a jest;
The virtuoso looks on me with scorn;
  But there's times when I am better than the best
Ask the stoker and the sailor of the sea;
  Ask the mucker and the hewer of the pine;
Ask the herder of the plain, ask the gleaner of the grain—
  There's a lowly, loving kingdom—and it's mine.

CLANCY OF THE MOUNTED POLICE

In the little Crimson Manual it's written plain and clear
That who would wear the scarlet coat shall say good-bye to
    fear;
Shall be a guardian of the right, a sleuth-hound of the trail—
In the little Crimson Manual there's no such word as "fail"—
Shall follow on though heavens fall, or hell's top-turrets freeze,
Half round the world, if need there be, on bleeding hands and
    knees.
It's duty, duty, first and last, the Crimson Manual saith;
The Scarlet Rider makes reply: "It's duty—to the death."
And so they sweep the solitudes, free men from all the earth;
And so they sentinel the woods, the wilds that know their
    worth;
And so they scour the startled plains and mock at hurt and pain,
And read their Crimson Manual, and find their duty plain.
Knights of the lists of unrenown, born of the frontier's need,
Disdainful of the spoken word, exultant in the deed;
Unconscious heroes of the waste, proud players of the game,
Props of the power behind the throne, upholders of the name:
For thus the Great White Chief hath said, "In all my lands be
    peace,"
And to maintain his word he gave his West the Scarlet Police.

Livid-lipped was the valley, still as the grave of God;
  Misty shadows of mountain thinned into mists of cloud;
Corpselike and stark was the land, with a quiet that crushed and
    awed,
  And the stars of the weird sub-arctic glimmered over its
    shroud.

Deep in the trench of the valley two men stationed the Post,
    Seymour and Clancy the reckless, fresh from the long patrol;
Seymour, the sergeant, and Clancy—Clancy who made his boast
    He could cinch like a bronco the Northland, and cling to the
        prongs of the Pole.

Two lone men on detachment, standing for law on the trail;
    Undismayed in the vastness, wise with the wisdom of old—
Out of the night hailed a half-breed telling a pitiful tale,
    "White man starving and crazy on the banks of the Norden-
        scold."

Up sprang the red-haired Clancy, lean and eager of eye;
    Loaded the long toboggan, strapped each dog at its post;
Whirled his lash at the leader; then, with a whoop and a cry,
    Into the Great White Silence faded away like a ghost.

The clouds were a misty shadow, the hills were a shadowy mist;
    Sunless, voiceless and pulseless, the day was a dream of woe;
Through the ice-rifts the river smoked and bubbled and hissed;
    Behind was a trail fresh broken, in front the untrodden snow.

Ahead of the dogs ploughed Clancy, haloed by steaming breath;
    Through peril of open water, through ache of insensate cold;
Up rivers wantonly winding in a land affianced to death,
    Till he came to a cowering cabin on the banks of the Norden-
        scold.

Then Clancy loosed his revolver, and he strode through the
        open door;
    And there was the man he sought for, crouching beside the
        fire;

The hair of his beard was singeing, the frost on his back was
  hoar,
  And ever he crooned and chanted as if he never would tire:—

*"I panned and I panned in the shiny sand, and I sniped on the
  river bar;*
*But I know, I know, that it's down below that the golden treas-
  ures are;*
*So I'll wait and wait till the floods abate, and I'll sink a shaft once
  more,*
*And I'd like to bet that I'll go home yet with a brass band play-
  ing before."*

He was nigh as thin as a sliver, and he whined like a Moose-hide
  cur;
  So Clancy clothed him and nursed him as a mother nurses a
  child;
Lifted him on the toboggan, wrapped him in robes of fur,
  Then with the dogs sore straining started to face the Wild.

Said the Wild, "I will crush this Clancy, so fearless and insolent;
  For him will I loose my fury, and blind and buffet and beat;
Pile up my snows to stay him; then when his strength is spent,
  Leap on him from my ambush and crush him under my feet.

"Him will I ring with my silence, compass him with my cold;
  Closer and closer clutch him unto mine icy breast;
Buffet him with my blizzards, deep in my snows enfold,
  Claiming his life as my tribute, giving my wolves the rest."

Clancy crawled through the vastness; o'er him the hate of the
  Wild;
  Full on his face fell the blizzard; cheering his huskies he ran;

Fighting, fierce-hearted and tireless, snows that drifted and
    piled,
  With ever and ever behind him singing the crazy man.

> *"Sing hey, sing ho, for the ice and snow,*
>   *And a heart that's ever merry;*
> *Let us trim and square with a lover's care*
>   *(For why should a man be sorry?)*
> *A grave deep, deep, with the moon a-peep,*
>   *A grave in the frozen mould.*
> *Sing hey, sing ho, for the winds that blow,*
> *And a grave deep down in the ice and snow,*
>   *A grave in the land of gold."*

Day after day of darkness, the whirl of the seething snows;
  Day after day of blindness, the swoop of the stinging blast;
On through a blur of fury the swing of staggering blows;
  On through a world of turmoil, empty, inane and vast.

Night with its writhing storm-whirl, night despairingly black;
  Night with its hours of terror, numb and endlessly long;
Night with its weary waiting, fighting the shadows back.
  And ever the crouching madman singing his crazy song.

Cold with its creeping terror, cold with its sudden clinch;
  Cold so utter you wonder if 'twill ever again be warm;
Clancy grinned as he shuddered, "Surely it isn't a cinch
  Being wet-nurse to a loony in the teeth of an arctic storm."

The blizzard passed and the dawn broke, knife-edged and crys-
    tal clear;
  The sky was a blue-domed iceberg, sunshine outlawed away;

Ever by snowslide and ice-rip haunted and hovered the Fear;
  Ever the Wild malignant poised and panted to slay.

The lead-dog freezes in harness—cut him out of the team!
  The lung of the wheel-dog's bleeding—shoot him and let
      him lie!
On and on with the others—lash them until they scream!
  "Pull for your lives, you devils! On! To halt is to die."

There in the frozen vastness Clancy fought with his foes;
  The ache of the stiffened fingers, the cut of the snowshoe
      thong;
Cheeks black-raw through the hood-flap, eyes that tingled and
    closed,
  And ever to urge and cheer him quavered the madman's song.

Colder it grew and colder, till the last heat left the earth,
  And there in the great stark stillness the balefires glinted and
      gleamed,
And the Wild all around exulted and shook with a devilish mirth,
  And life was far and forgotten, the ghost of a joy once
      dreamed.

Death! And one who defied it, a man of the Mounted Police;
  Fought it there to a standstill long after hope was gone;
Grinned through his bitter anguish, fought without let or cease,
  Suffering, straining, striving, stumbling, struggling on.

Till the dogs lay down in their traces, and rose and staggered
    and fell;
  Till the eyes of him dimmed with shadows, and the trail was
      so hard to see;

Till the Wild howled out triumphant, and the world was a
  frozen hell—
  Then said Constable Clancy: "I guess that it's up to me."

Far down the trail they saw him, and his hands they were
  blanched like bone;
  His face was a blackened horror, from his eyelids the salt
    rheum ran;
His feet he was lifting strangely, as if they were made of stone,
  But safe in his arms and sleeping he carried the crazy man.

So Clancy got into Barracks, and the boys made rather a scene;
  And the O. C. called him a hero, and was nice as a man
    could be;
But Clancy gazed down his trousers at the place where his toes
  had been,
  And then he howled like a husky, and sang in a shaky key.

"When I go back to the old love that's true to the finger-tips,
I'll say: 'Here's bushels of gold, love,' and I'll kiss my girl on the
  lips;
'It's yours to have and to hold, love.' It's the proud, proud boy
  I'll be,
When I go back to the old love that's waited so long for me."

THE LAND OF BEYOND

Have ever you heard of the Land of Beyond,
    That dreams at the gates of the day?
Alluring it lies at the skirts of the skies,
    And ever so far away;
Alluring it calls: O ye the yoke galls,
    And ye of the trail overfond,
With saddle and pack, by paddle and track,
    Let's go to the Land of Beyond!

Have ever you stood where the silences brood,
    And vast the horizons begin,
At the dawn of the day to behold far away
    The goal you would strive for and win?
Yet ah! in the night when you gain to the height,
    With the vast pool of heaven star-spawned,
Afar and agleam, like a valley of dream,
    Still mocks you a Land of Beyond.

Thank God! there is always a Land of Beyond
    For us who are true to the trail;
A vision to seek, a beckoning peak,
    A fairness that never will fail;
A pride in our soul that mocks at a goal,
    A manhood that irks at a bond,
And try how we will, unattainable still,
    Behold it, our Land of Beyond!

ATHABASKA DICK

When the boys come out from Lac Labiche in the lure of the
    early Spring,
To take the pay of the "Hudson's Bay," as their fathers did
    before,
They are all a-glee for the jamboree, and they make the Landing
    ring
With a whoop and a whirl, and a "Grab your girl," and a rip
    and a skip and a roar.
For the spree of Spring is a sacred thing, and the boys must have
    their fun;
Packer and tracker and half-breed Cree, from the boat to the
    bar they leap;
And then when the long flotilla goes, and the last of their pay
    is done,
The boys from the banks of Lac Labiche swing to the heavy
    sweep.
And oh, how they sigh! and their throats are dry, and sorry are
    they and sick:
Yet there's none so cursed with a lime-kiln thirst as that Atha-
    baska Dick.

He was long and slim and lean of limb, but strong as a stripling
    bear;
And by the right of his skill and might he guided the Long
    Brigade.
All water-wise were his laughing eyes, and he steered with a
    careless care,
And he shunned the shock of foam and rock, till they came to
    the Big Cascade.

And here they must make the long *portăge*, and the boys sweat
    in the sun;
And they heft and pack, and they haul and track, and each must
    do his trick;
But their thoughts are far in the Landing bar, where the founts
    of nectar run:
And no man thinks of such gorgeous drinks as that Athabaska
    Dick.

'Twas the close of day and his long boat lay just over the Big
    Cascade,
When there came to him one Jack-pot Jim, with a wild light in
    his eye;
And he softly laughed, and he led Dick aft, all eager, yet half
    afraid,
And snugly stowed in his coat he showed a pilfered flask of
    "rye."
And in haste he slipped, or in fear he tripped, but—Dick in
    warning roared—
And there rang a yell, and it befell that Jim was overboard.

Oh, I heard a splash, and quick as a flash I knew he could not
    swim.
I saw him whirl in the river swirl, and thresh his arms about.
In a queer, strained way I heard Dick say: "I'm going after him,"
Throw off his coat, leap down the boat—and then I gave a shout:
"Boys, grab him, quick! You're crazy, Dick! Far better one
    than two!
"Hell, man! You know you've got no show! It's sure and certain
    death. . . ."
And there we hung, and there we clung, with beef and brawn
    and thew,

And sinews cracked and joints were racked, and panting came
 our breath;
And there we swayed and there we prayed, till strength and
 hope were spent—
Then Dick, he threw us off like rats, and after Jim he went.

With mighty urge amid the surge of river-rage he leapt,
And gripped his mate and desperate he fought to gain the shore;
With teeth a-gleam he bucked the stream, yet swift and sure he
 swept
To meet the mighty cataract that waited all a-roar.
And there we stood like carven wood, our faces sickly white,
And watched him as he beat the foam, and inch by inch he lost;
And nearer, nearer drew the fall, and fiercer grew the fight,
Till on the very cascade crest a last farewell he tossed.
Then down and down and down they plunged into that pit of
 dread;
And mad we tore along the shore to claim our bitter dead.

And from that hell of frenzied foam, that crashed and fumed
 and boiled,
Two little bodies bubbled up, and they were heedless then;
And oh, they lay like senseless clay! and bitter hard we toiled,
Yet never, never gleam of hope, and we were weary men.
And moments mounted into hours, and black was our despair;
And faint were we, and we were fain to give them up as dead,
When suddenly I thrilled with hope: "Back, boys! and give
 him air;
"I feel the flutter of his heart. . . ." And, as the word I said,
Dick gave a sigh, and gazed around, and saw our breathless
 band;
And saw the sky's blue floor above, all strewn with golden
 fleece;

And saw his comrade Jack-pot Jim, and touched him with his
    hand:
And then there came into his eyes a look of perfect peace.
And as there, at his very feet, the thwarted river raved,
I heard him murmur low and deep:
      "Thank God! the *whiskey's* saved."

THE ROVER

I

Oh, how good it is to be
Foot-loose and heart-free!
Just my dog and pipe and I, underneath the vast sky;
Trail to try and goal to win, white road and cool inn;
Fields to lure a lad afar, clear spring and still star;
Lilting feet that never tire, green dingle, fagot fire;
None to hurry, none to hold, heather hill and hushed fold;
Nature like a picture book, laughing leaf and bright brook;
Every day a jewel bright, set serenely in the night;
Every night a holy shrine, radiant for a day divine.

Weathered cheek and kindly eye, let the wanderer go by.
Woman-love and wistful heart, let the gipsy one depart.
For the farness and the road are his glory and his goad.
Oh, the lilt of youth and Spring! Eyes laugh and lips sing.
Yea, but it is good to be
Foot-loose and heart-free!

II

Yet how good it is to come
Home at last, home, home!
On the clover swings the bee, overhead's the hale tree;
Sky of turquoise gleams through, yonder glints the lake's blue.
In a hammock let's swing, weary of wandering;
Tired of wild, uncertain lands, strange faces, faint hands.

Has the wondrous world gone cold? Am I growing old, old?
Grey and weary . . . let me dream, glide on the tranquil stream.
Oh, what joyous days I've had, full, fervid, gay, glad!
Yet there comes a subtile change, let the stripling rove, range.
From sweet roving comes sweet rest, after all, home's best.
And if there's a little bit of woman-love with it,
I will count my life content, God-blest and well spent. . . .

        Oh but it is good to be
        Foot-loose and heart-free!
        Yet how good it is to come
        Home at last, home, home!

JUST THINK!

Just think! some night the stars will gleam
   Upon a cold, grey stone,
And trace a name with silver beam,
   And lo! 'twill be your own.

That night is speeding on to greet
   Your epitaphic rhyme.
You life is but a little beat
   Within the heart of Time.

A little gain, a little pain,
   A laugh, lest you may moan;
A little blame, a little fame,
   A star-gleam on a stone.

THE MOUNTAIN AND THE LAKE

I KNOW a mountain thrilling to the stars,
Peerless and pure, and pinnacled with snow;
Glimpsing the golden dawn o'er coral bars,
Flaunting the vanisht sunset's garnet glow;
Proudly patrician, passionless, serene;
Soaring in silvered steeps where cloud-surfs break;
Virgin and vestal— Oh, a very Queen!
And at her feet there dreams a quiet lake.

My lake adores my mountain—well I know,
For I have watched it from its dawn-dream start,
Stilling its mirror to her splendid snow,
Framing her image in its trembling heart;
Glassing her graciousness of greening wood,
Kissing her throne, melodiously mad,
Thrilling responsive to her every mood,
Gloomed with her sadness, gay when she is glad.

My lake has dreamed and loved since time was born;
Will love and dream till time shall cease to be;
Gazing to Her in worship half forlorn,
Who looks towards the stars and will not see—
My peerless mountain, splendid in her scorn. . . .
Alas! poor little lake! Alas! poor me!

THE QUITTER

WHEN you're lost in the Wild, and you're scared as a child,
　　And Death looks you bang in the eye,
And you're sore as a boil, it's according to Hoyle
　　To cock your revolver and . . . die.
But the Code of a Man says: "Fight all you can,"
　　And self-dissolution is barred.
In hunger and woe, oh, it's easy to blow . . .
　　It's the hell-served-for-breakfast that's hard.

"You're sick of the game!" Well, now, that's a shame.
　　You're young and you're brave and you're bright.
"You've had a raw deal!" I know—but don't squeal,
　　Buck up, do your damnedest, and fight.
It's the plugging away that will win you the day,
　　So don't be a piker, old pard!
Just draw on your grit; it's so easy to quit:
　　It's the keeping-your-chin-up that's hard.

It's easy to cry that you're beaten—and die;
　　It's easy to crawfish and crawl;
But to fight and to fight when hope's out of sight—
　　Why, that's the best game of them all!
And though you come out of each gruelling bout,
　　All broken and beaten and scarred,
Just have one more try—it's dead easy to die,
　　It's the keeping-on-living that's hard.

WHILE THE BANNOCK BAKES

Light up your pipe again, old chum, and sit awhile with me;
I've got to watch the bannock bake—how restful is the air!
You'd little think that we were somewhere north of Sixty-three,
Though where I don't exactly know, and don't precisely care.
The man-size mountains palisade us round on every side;
The river is a-flop with fish, and ripples silver-clear;
The midnight sunshine brims yon cleft—we think it's the Di-
    vide;
We'll get there in a month, maybe, or maybe in a year.

It doesn't matter, does it, pal? We're of that breed of men
With whom the world of wine and cards and women disagree;
Your trouble was a roofless game of poker now and then,
And "raising up my elbow," that's what got away with me.
We're merely "Undesirables," artistic more or less;
My horny hands are Chopin-wise; you quote your Browning
    well;
And yet we're fooling round for gold in this damned wilderness:
The joke is, if we found it, we would both go straight to hell.

Well, maybe we won't find it—and at least we've got the "life."
We're both as brown as berries, and could wrestle with a bear:
(That bannock's raising nicely, pal, just jab it with your knife.)
Fine specimens of manhood they would reckon us out there
It's the tracking and the packing and the poling in the sun;
It's the sleeping in the open, it's the rugged, unfaked food;
It's the snow-shoe and the paddle, and the camp-fire and the gun,
And when I think of what I was, I know that it is good.

79

Just think of how we've poled all day up this strange little
    stream;
Since life began no eye of man has seen this place before;
How fearless all the wild things are! the banks with goose-grass
    gleam,
And there's a bronzy musk-rat sitting sniffing at his door.
A mother duck with brood of ten comes squattering along;
The tawny, white-winged ptarmigan are flying all about;
And in that swirly, golden pool, a restless, gleaming throng,
The trout are waiting till we condescend to take them out.

Ah, yes, it's good! I'll bet that there's no doctor like the Wild:
(Just turn that bannock over there; it's getting nicely brown.)
I might be in my grave by now, forgotten and reviled,
Or rotting like a sickly cur in some far, foreign town.
I might be that vile thing I was,—it all seems like a dream;
I owed a man a grudge one time that only life could pay;
And yet it's half-forgotten now—how petty these things seem!
(But that's "another story," pal; I'll tell it you some day.)

How strange two "irresponsibles" should chum away up here!
But round the Arctic Circle friends are few and far between
We've shared the same camp-fire and tent for nigh on seven
    year,
And never had a word that wasn't cheering and serene.
We've halved the toil and split the spoil, and borne each other's
    packs;
By all the Wild's freemasonry we're brothers, tried and true;
We've swept on danger side by side, and fought it back to back.
And you would die for me, old pal, and I would die for you.

Now there was that time I got lost in Rory Bory Land,
(How quick the blizzards sweep on one across that Polar sea!)

You formed a rescue crew of One, and saw a frozen hand
That stuck out of a drift of snow—and, partner, it was Me.
But I got even, did I not, that day the paddle broke?
White water on the Coppermine—a rock—a split canoe—
Two fellows struggling in the foam (one couldn't swim a
  stroke):
A half-drowned man I dragged ashore . . . and partner, it was
  You.

* * * * * * * * *

In Rory Borealis Land the winter's long and black.
The silence seems a solid thing, shot through with wolfish woe;
And rowelled by the eager stars the skies vault vastly back,
And man seems but a little mite on that weird-lit plateau.
Nothing to do but smoke and yarn of wild and misspent lives,
Beside the camp-fire there we sat—what tales you told to me
Of love and hate, and chance and fate, and temporary wives!
In Rory Borealis Land, beside the Arctic Sea.

One yarn you told me in those days I can remember still;
It seemed as if I visioned it, so sharp you sketched it in;
Bellona was the name, I think; a coast town in Brazil,
Where nobody did anything but serenade and sin.
I saw it all—the jewelled sea, the golden scythe of sand,
The stately pillars of the palms, the feathery bamboo,
The red-roofed houses and the swart, sun-dominated land,
The people ever children, and the heavens ever blue.

You told me of that girl of yours, that blossom of old Spain,
All glamour, grace and witchery, all passion, verve and glow.
How maddening she must have been! You made me see her
  plain,
There by our little camp-fire, in the silence and the snow.

You loved her and she loved you. She'd a husband, too, I think,
A doctor chap, you told me, whom she treated like a dog,
A white man living on the beach, a hopeless slave to drink—
(Just turn that bannock over there, that's propped against the
    log.)

That story seemed to strike me, pal—it happens every day:
You had to go away awhile, then somehow it befell
The doctor chap discovered, gave her up, and disappeared;
You came back, tired of her in time . . . there's nothing more
    to tell.
Hist! see those willows silvering where swamp and river meet!
Just reach me up my rifle quick; that's Mister Moose, I know—
There now, *I've got him dead to rights* . . . but hell! we've lots
    to eat
I don't believe in taking life—we'll let the beggar go.

Heigh ho! I'm tired; the bannock's cooked; it's time we both
    turned in.
The morning mist is coral-kissed, the morning sky is gold.
The camp-fire's a confessional—what funny yarns we spin!
It sort of made me think a bit, that story that you told.
The fig-leaf belt and Rory Bory are such odd extremes,
Yet after all how very small this old world seems to be . . .
Yes, that was quite a yarn, old pal, and yet to me it seems
You missed the point: the point is that the "doctor chap" . . .
    was ME. . . .

THE LOST MASTER

"AND when I come to die," he said,
"Ye shall not lay me out in state,
Nor leave your laurels at my head,
Nor cause your men of speech orate;
No monument your gift shall be,
No column in the Hall of Fame;
But just this line ye grave for me:
    'He played the game.' "

So when his glorious task was done,
It was not of his fame we thought;
It was not of his battles won,
But of the pride with which he fought;
But of his zest, his ringing laugh,
His trenchant scorn of praise or blame:
And so we graved his epitaph,
    "He played the game."

And so we, too, in humbler ways
Went forth to fight the fight anew,
And heeding neither blame nor praise,
We held the course he set us true.
And we, too, find the fighting sweet;
And we, too, fight for fighting's sake;
And though we go down in defeat,
And though our stormy hearts may break,
We will not do our Master shame:
We'll play the game, please God,
    We'll play the game.

THE WANDERLUST

THE Wanderlust has lured me to the seven lonely seas,
Has dumped me on the tailing-piles of dearth;
The Wanderlust has haled me from the morris chair of ease,
Has hurled me to the ends of all the earth.
How bitterly I've cursed it, oh, the Painted Desert knows,
The wraithlike heights that hug the pallid plain,
The all-but-fluid silence,—yet the longing grows and grows,
And I've got to glut the Wanderlust again.

Soldier, sailor, in what a plight I've been!
Tinker, tailor, oh what a sight I've seen!
And I'm hitting the trail in the morning, boys,
And you won't see my heels for dust;
For it's "all day" with you
When you answer the cue
        Of the Wan-der-lust.

The Wanderlust has got me . . . by the belly-aching fire,
By the fever and the freezing and the pain;
By the darkness that just drowns you, by the wail of home de-
        sire,
I've tried to break the spell of it—in vain.
Life might have been a feast for me, now there are only crumbs;
In rags and tatters, beggar-wise I sit;
Yet there's no rest or peace for me, imperious it drums,
The Wanderlust, and I must follow it.

Highway, by-way, many a mile I've done;
Rare way, fair way, many a height I've won;

But I'm pulling my freight in the morning, boys,
And it's over the hills or bust;
For there's never a cure
When you list to the lure
   Of the Wan-der-lust.

The Wanderlust has taught me . . . it has whispered to my heart
Things all you stay-at-homes will never know.
The white man and the savage are but three short days apart,
Three days of cursing, crawling, doubt and woe.
Then it's down to chewing muclucs, to the water you can *eat*,
To fish you bolt with nose held in your hand.
When you get right down to cases, it's King's Grub that rules the races,
And the Wanderlust will help you understand.

Haunting, taunting, that is the spell of it;
Mocking, baulking, that is the hell of it;
But I'll shoulder my pack in the morning, boys,
And I'm going because I must;
For it's so-long to all
When you answer the call
   Of the Wan-der-lust.

The Wanderlust has blest me . . . in a ragged blanket curled,
I've watched the gulf of Heaven foam with stars;
I've walked with eyes wide open to the wonder of the world,
I've seen God's flood of glory burst its bars.
I've seen the gold a-blinding in the riffles of the sky,
Till I fancied me a bloated plutocrat;
But I'm freedom's happy bond-slave, and I will be till I die,
And I've got to thank the Wanderlust for that.

Wild heart, child heart, all of the world your home.
Glad heart, mad heart, what can you do but roam?
Oh, I'll beat it once more in the morning, boys,
With a pinch of tea and a crust;
For you cannot deny
When you hark to the cry
        Of the Wan-der-lust.

The Wanderlust will claim me at the finish for its own.
I'll turn my back on men and face the Pole.
Beyond the Arctic outposts I will venture all alone;
Some Never-never Land will be my goal.
Thank God! there's none will miss me, for I've been a bird of
    flight;
And in my moccasins I'll take my call;
For the Wanderlust has ruled me,
And the Wanderlust has schooled me,
And I'm ready for the darkest trail of all.

Grim land, dim land, oh, how the vastness calls!
Far land, star land, oh, how the stillness falls!
For you never can tell if it's heaven or hell,
And I'm taking the trail on trust;
But I haven't a doubt
That my soul will leap out
        On its Wan-der-lust.

THE SQUAW MAN

THE cow-moose comes to water, and the beaver's overbold,
The net is in the eddy of the stream;
The teepee stars the vivid sward with russet, red and gold,
And in the velvet gloom the fire's a-gleam.
The night is ripe with quiet, rich with incense of the pine;
From sanctuary lake I hear the loon;
The peaks are bright against the blue, and drenched with sunset
    wine,
And like a silver bubble is the moon.

Cloud-high I climbed but yesterday; a hundred miles around
I looked to see a rival fire a-gleam,
As in a crystal lens it lay, a land without a bound,
All lure, and virgin vastitude, and dream.
The great sky soared exultantly, the great earth bared its breast,
All river-veined and patterned with the pine;
The heedless hordes of caribou were streaming to the West,
A land of lustrous mystery—and mine.

Yea, mine to frame my Odyssey: Oh, little do they know
My conquest and the kingdom that I keep!
The meadows of the musk-ox, where the laughing grasses grow,
The rivers where the careless conies leap.
Beyond the silent Circle, where white men are fierce and few,
I lord it, and I mock at man-made law;
Like a flame upon the water is my little light canoe,
And yonder in the fireglow is my squaw.

A squaw man! yes, that's what I am; sneer at me if you will.
I've gone the grilling pace that cannot last;
With bawdry, bridge and brandy— Oh, I've drunk enough to
　　kill
A dozen such as you, but that is past.
I've swung round to my senses, found the place where I belong;
The City made a madman out of me;
But here beyond the Circle, where there's neither right or
　　wrong,
I leap from life's strait-jacket, and I'm free.

Yet ever in the far forlorn, by trails of lone desire;
Yet ever in the dawn's white leer of hate;
Yet ever by the dripping kill, beside the drowsy fire,
There comes the fierce heart-hunger for a mate.
There comes the mad blood-clamour for a woman's clinging
　　hand,
Love-humid eyes, the velvet of a breast;
And so I sought the Bonnet-plumes, and chose from out the
　　band
The girl I thought the sweetest and the best.

O wistful women I have loved before my dark disgrace!
O women fair and rare in my home land!
Dear ladies, if I saw you now I'd turn away my face,
Then crawl to kiss your foot-prints in the sand!
And yet—that day the rifle jammed—a wounded moose at
　　bay—
A roar, a charge . . . I faced it with my knife:
A shot from out the willow-scrub, and there the monster
　　lay. . . .
Yes, little Laughing Eyes, you saved my life.

The man must have the woman, and we're all brutes more or less,
Since first the male ape shinned the family tree;
And yet I think I love her with a husband's tenderness,
And yet I know that she would die for me.
Oh, if I left you, Laughing Eyes, and nevermore came back,
God help you, girl! I know what you would do. . . .
I see the lake wan in the moon, and from the shadow black,
There drifts a little, *empty* birch canoe.

We're here beyond the Circle, where there's never wrong nor
    right;
We aren't spliced according to the law;
But by the gods I hail you on this hushed and holy night
As the mother of my children, and my squaw.
I see your little slender face set in the firelight glow;
I pray that I may never make it sad;
I hear you croon a baby song, all slumber-soft and low—
God bless you, little Laughing Eyes! I'm glad.

A SONG OF SUCCESS

Ho! we were strong, we were swift, we were brave.
Youth was a challenge, and Life was a fight.
All that was best in us gladly we gave,
Sprang from the rally, and leapt for the height.
Smiling is Love in a foam of Spring flowers:
Harden our hearts to him—on let us press!
Oh, what a triumph and pride shall be ours!
See where it beacons, the star of success!

Cares seem to crowd on us—so much to do;
New fields to conquer, and time's on the wing.
Grey hairs are showing, a wrinkle or two;
Somehow our footstep is losing its spring.
Pleasure's forsaken us, Love ceased to smile;
Youth has been funeralled; Age travels fast.
Sometimes we wonder: is it worth while?
There! we have gained to the summit at last.

Aye, we have triumphed! Now must we haste,
Revel in victory . . . why! what is wrong?
Life's choicest vintage is flat to the taste—
Are we too late? Have we laboured too long?
Wealth, power, fame we hold . . . ah! but the truth:
Would we not give this vain glory of ours
For one mad, glad year of glorious youth,
Life in the Springtide, and Love in the flowers.

THE LOGGER

In the moonless, misty night, with my little pipe alight,
    I am sitting by the camp-fire's fading cheer;
Oh, the dew is falling chill on the dim, deer-haunted hill,
    And the breakers in the bay are moaning drear.
The toilful hours are sped, the boys are long abed,
    And I alone a weary vigil keep;
In the sightless, sullen sky I can hear the night-hawk cry,
    And the frogs in frenzied chorus from the creek.

And somehow the embers' glow brings me back the long ago,
    The days of merry laughter and light song;
When I sped the hours away with the gayest of the gay
    In the giddy whirl of fashion's festal throng.
Oh, I ran a grilling race and I little recked the pace,
    For the lust of youth ran riot in my blood;
But at last I made a stand in this God-forsaken land
    Of the pine-tree and the mountain and the flood.

And now I've got to stay, with an overdraft to pay,
    For pleasure in the past with future pain;
And I'm not the chap to whine, for if the chance were mine
    I know I'd choose the old life once again.
With its woman's eyes a-shine, and its flood of golden wine,
    Its fever and its frolic and its fun;
The old life with its din, its laughter and its sin—
    And chuck me in the gutter when it's done.

Ah, well! it's past and gone, and the memory is wan,
    That conjures up each old familiar face;

And here by fortune hurled, I am dead to all the world,
　　And I've learned to lose my pride and keep my place.
My ways are hard and rough, and my arms are strong and tough,
　　And I hew the dizzy pine till darkness falls;
And sometimes I take a dive, just to keep my heart alive,
　　Among the gay saloons and dancing halls.

In the distant, dinful town just a little drink to drown
　　The cares that crowd and canker in my brain;
Just a little joy to still set my pulses all a-thrill,
　　Then back to brutish labour once again.
And things will go on so until one day I shall know
　　That Death has got me cinched beyond a doubt;
Then I'll crawl away from sight, and morosely in the night
　　My weary, wasted life will peter out.

Then the boys will gather round, and they'll launch me in the
　　　ground,
　　And pile the stones the timber wolf to foil;
And the moaning pine will wave overhead a nameless grave,
　　Where the black snake in the sunshine loves to coil.
And they'll leave me there alone, and perhaps with softened tone
　　Speak of me sometimes in the camp-fire's glow,
As a played-out, broken chum, who has gone to Kingdom
　　　Come,
　　And who went the pace in England long ago.

HEART O' THE NORTH

AND when I come to the dim trail-end,
    I who have been Life's rover,
This is all I would ask, my friend,
    Over and over and over:

A little space on a stony hill
    With never another near me,
Sky o' the North that's vast and still,
    With a single star to cheer me;

Star that gleams on a moss-grey stone
    Graven by those who love me—
There would I lie alone, alone,
    With a single pine above me;

Pine that the north wind whinnys through—
    Oh, I have been Life's lover!
But there I'd lie and listen to
    Eternity passing over.

FUNK

When your marrer bone seems 'oller,
And you're glad you ain't no taller,
And you're all a-shakin' like you 'ad the chills;
When your skin creeps like a pullet's,
And you're duckin' all the bullets,
And you're green as gorgonzola round the gills;
When your legs seem made of jelly,
And you're squeamish in the belly,
And you want to turn about and do a bunk:
For Gawd's sake, kid, don't show it!
Don't let your mateys know it—
You're just sufferin' from funk, funk, funk.

Of course there's no denyin'
That it ain't so easy tryin'
To grin and grip your rifle by the butt,
When the 'ole world rips asunder,
And you sees yer pal go under,
As a bunch of shrapnel sprays 'im on the nut;
I admit it's 'ard contrivin'
When you 'ears the shells arrivin',
To discover you're a bloomin' bit o' spunk;
But, my lad, you've got to do it,
And your God will see you through it,
For wot 'E 'ates is funk, funk, funk.

So stand up, son; look gritty,
And just 'um a lively ditty,
And only be afraid to be afraid;

Just 'old yer rifle steady,
And 'ave yer bay'nit ready,
For that's the way good soldier-men is made.
And if you 'as to die,
As it sometimes 'appens, why,
Far better die a 'ero than a skunk;
A-doin' of yer bit,
And so—to 'ell with it,
There ain't no bloomin' funk, funk, funk.

GOING HOME

I'M goin' 'ome to Blighty—ain't I glad to 'ave the chance!
I'm loaded up wiv fightin', and I've 'ad my fill o' France;
I'm feelin' so excited-like, I want to sing and dance,
 For I'm goin' 'ome to Blighty in the mawnin'.

I'm goin' 'ome to Blighty: can you wonder as I'm gay?
I've got a wound I wouldn't sell for 'alf a year o' pay;
A harm that's mashed to jelly in the nicest sort o' way,
 For it takes me 'ome to Blighty in the mawnin'.

'Ow everlastin' keen I was on gettin' to the front!
I'd ginger for a dozen, and I 'elped to bear the brunt;
But Cheese and Crust! I'm crazy, now I've done me little stunt,
 To sniff the air of Blighty in the mawnin'.

I've looked upon the wine that's white, and on the wine that's
  red;
I've looked on cider flowin', till it fairly turned me 'ead;
But oh, the finest scoff will be, when all is done and said,
 A pint o' Bass in Blighty in the mawnin'.

I'm goin' back to Blighty, which I left to strafe the 'Un;
I've fought in bloody battles, and I've 'ad a 'eap of fun;
But now me flipper's busted, and I think me dooty's done,
 And I'll kiss me gel in Blighty in the mawnin'.

Oh, there be furrin lands to see, and some of 'em be fine;
And there be furrin gels to kiss, and scented furrin wine;
But there's no land like England, and no other gel like mine:
 Thank Gawd for dear old Blighty in the mawnin'.

BILL THE BOMBER

THE poppies gleamed like bloody pools through cotton-woolly
    mist;
The Captain kept a-lookin' at the watch upon his wrist;
And there we smoked and squatted, as we watched the shrapnel
    flame;
'Twas wonnerful, I'm tellin' you, how fast them bullets came.
'Twas weary work the waiting, though; I tried to sleep a wink,
For waitin' means a-thinkin', and it doesn't do to think.
So I closed my eyes a little, and I had a niceish dream
Of a-standin' by a dresser with a dish of Devon cream;
But I hadn't time to sample it, for suddenlike I woke:
"Come on, me lads!" the Captain says, 'n I climbed out through
    the smoke.

We spread out in the open: it was like a bath of lead;
But the boys they cheered and hollered fit to raise the bloody
    dead,
Till a beastly bullet copped 'em, then they lay without a sound,
And it's odd—we didn't seem to heed them corpses on the
    ground.
And I kept on thinkin', thinkin', as the bullets faster flew,
How they picks the werry best men, and they lets the rotters
    through;
So indiscriminatin' like, they spares a man of sin,
And a rare lad wot's a husband and a father gets done in.
And while havin' these reflections and advancin' on the run,
A bullet biffs me shoulder, and says I: "That's number one."

Well, it downed me for a jiffy, but I didn't lose me calm,
For I knew that I was needed: I'm a bomber, so I am.

I 'ad lost me cap and rifle, but I "carried on" because
I 'ad me bombs and knew that they was needed, so they was.
We didn't 'ave no singin' now, nor many men to cheer;
Maybe the shrapnel drowned 'em, crashin' out so werry near;
And the Maxims got us sideways, and the bullets faster flew,
And I copped one on me flipper, and says I: "That's number
two."

I was pleased it was the left one, for I 'ad me bombs, ye see.
And 'twas 'ard if they'd be wasted like, and all along o' me.
And I'd lost me 'at and rifle—but I told you that before,
So I packed me mit inside me coat and "carried on" once more.
But the rumpus it was wicked, and the men were scarcer yet,
And I felt me ginger goin', but me jaws I kindo set,
And we passed the Boche first trenches, which was 'eapin' 'igh
with dead,
And we started for their second, which was fifty feet ahead;
When something like a 'ammer smashed me savage on the knee,
And down I came all muck and blood: Says I: "That's number
three."

So there I lay all 'elpless like, and bloody sick at that,
And worryin' like anythink, because I'd lost me 'at;
And thinkin' of me missis, and the partin' words she said:
"If you gets killed, write quick, ol' man, and tell me as you're
dead."
And lookin' at me bunch o' bombs—that was the 'ardest blow,
To think I'd never 'ave the chance to 'url them at the foe.
And there was all our boys in front, a-fightin' there like mad,
And me as could 'ave 'elped 'em wiv the lovely bombs I 'ad.
And so I cussed and cussed, and then I struggled back again,
Into that bit of battered trench, packed solid with its slain.

Now as I lay a-lyin' there and blastin' of me lot,
And wishin' I could just dispose of all them bombs I'd got,
I sees within the doorway of a shy, retirin' dug-out
Six Boches all a-grinnin', and their Captain stuck 'is mug out;
And they 'ad a nice machine gun, and I twigged what they was
    at;
And they fixed it on a tripod, and I watched 'em like a cat;
And they got it in position, and they seemed so werry glad,
Like they'd got us in a death-trap, which, condemn their souls!
    they 'ad.
For there our boys was fightin' fifty yards in front, and 'ere
This lousy bunch of Boches they 'ad got us in the rear.

Oh, it set me blood a-boilin' and I quite forgot me pain,
So I started crawlin', crawlin' over all them mounds of slain;
And them barstards was so busy-like they 'ad no eyes for me,
And me bleedin' leg was draggin', but me right arm it was
    free. . . .
And now they 'ave it all in shape, and swingin' sweet and clear;
And now they're all excited like, but—I am drawin' near;
And now they 'ave it loaded up, and now they're takin'
    aim. . . .
Rat-tat-tat-tat! Oh, here, says I, is where I join the game.
And my right arm it goes swingin', and a bomb it goes a-slingin',
And that "typewriter" goes wingin' in a thunderbolt of flame.

Then these Boches, wot was left of 'em, they tumbled down
    their 'ole,
And up I climbed a mound of dead, and down on them I stole.
And, oh, that blessed moment when I heard their frightened yell,
And I laughed down in that dug-out, ere I bombed their souls
    to hell.

And now I'm in the hospital, surprised that I'm alive;
We started out a thousand men, we came back thirty-five.
And I'm minus of a trotter, but I'm most amazin' gay,
For me bombs they wasn't wasted, though, you might say,
 "thrown away."

MY JOB

I'VE got a little job on 'and, the time is drawin' nigh;
At seven by the Captain's watch I'm due to go and do it;
I wants to 'ave it nice and neat, and pleasin' to the eye,
And I 'opes the God of soldier men will see me safely through it.
Because, you see, it's somethin' I 'ave never done before;
And till you 'as experience noo stunts is always tryin';
The chances is I'll never 'ave to do it any more:
At seven by the Captain's watch my little job is . . . *dyin'*.

I've got a little note to write; I'd best begin it now.
I ain't much good at writin' notes, but here goes: "Dearest
    Mother,
I've been in many 'ot old 'do's'; I've scraped through safe
    some'ow,
But now I'm on the very point of tacklin' another.
A little job of hand-grenades; they called for volunteers.
They picked me out; I'm proud of it; it seems a trifle dicky.
If anythin' should 'appen, well, there ain't no call for tears,
And so . . . I 'opes this finds you well.—Your werry lovin'
    Micky."

I've got a little score to settle wiv them swine out there.
I've 'ad so many of me pals done in it's quite upset me.
I've seen so much of bloody death I don't seem for to care,
If I can only even up, how soon the blighters get me.
I'm sorry for them perishers that corpses in a bed;
I only 'opes mine's short and sweet, no linger-longer-lyin';
I've made a mess of life, but now I'll try to make instead . . .
It's seven sharp. Good-bye, old pals! . . . *a decent job in dyin'*.

THE TWINS

THERE were two brothers, John and James,
And when the town went up in flames,
To save the house of James dashed John,
Then turned, and lo! his own was gone.

And when the great World War began,
To volunteer John promptly ran;
And while he learned live bombs to lob,
James stayed at home and—sneaked his job.

John came home with a missing limb;
That didn't seem to worry him;
But oh, it set his brain awhirl
To find that James had—sneaked his girl!

Time passed. John tried his grief to drown;
To-day James owns one-half the town;
His army contracts riches yield;
And John? Well, *search the Potter's Field.*

L'ESCARGOT D'OR

O TAVERN of the Golden Snail!
Ten *sous* have I, so I'll regale;
Ten *sous* your amber brew to sip
(Eight for the *bock* and two the tip),
And so I'll sit the evening long,
And smoke my pipe and watch the throng,
The giddy crowd that drains and drinks,
I'll watch it quiet as a sphinx;
And who among them all shall buy
For ten poor *sous* such joy as I?
As I who, snugly tucked away,
Look on it all as on a play,
A frolic scene of love and fun,
To please an audience of One.

O Tavern of the Golden Snail!
You've stuff indeed for many a tale.
All eyes, all ears, I nothing miss:
Two lovers lean to clasp and kiss;
The merry students sing and shout,
The nimble *garçons* dart about;
Lo! here come Mimi and Musette
With: *"S'il vous plait, une cigarette?"*
Marcel and Rudolf, Schaunard too,
Behold the old rapscallion crew,
With flowing tie and shaggy head . . .
Who says Bohemia is dead?
Oh shades of Murger! prank and clown,
And I will watch and write it down.

O Tavern of the Golden Snail!
What crackling throats have gulped your ale!
What sons of Fame from far and near
Have glowed and mellowed in your cheer!
Within this corner where I sit
Banville and Coppée clashed their wit;
And hither too, to dream and drain,
And drown despair, came poor Verlaine.
Here Wilde would talk and Synge would muse,
Maybe like me with just ten *sous*.
Ah! one is lucky, is one not?
With ghosts so rare to drain a pot!
So may your custom never fail,
O Tavern of the Golden Snail!

IT IS LATER THAN YOU THINK

Lone amid the café's cheer,
Sad of heart am I to-night;
Dolefully I drink my beer,
But no single line I write.
There's the wretched rent to pay,
Yet I glower at pen and ink:
Oh, inspire me, Muse, I pray,
It is later than you think!

Hello! there's a pregnant phrase.
Bravo! let me write it down;
Hold it with a hopeful gaze,
Gauge it with a fretful frown;
Tune it to my lyric lyre . . .
Ah! upon starvation's brink,
How the words are dark and dire:
It is later than you think.

Weigh them well. . . . Behold yon **band**,
Students drinking by the door,
Madly merry, *bock* in hand,
Saucers stacked to mark their score.
Get you gone, you jolly scamps;
Let your parting glasses clink;
Seek your long neglected lamps:
It is later than you think.

Look again: yon dainty blonde,
All allure and golden grace,

Oh so willing to respond
Should you turn a smiling face.
Play your part, poor pretty doll;
Feast and frolic, pose and prink;
There's the Morgue to end it all,
And it's later than you think.

Yon's a playwright—mark his face,
Puffed and purple, tense and tired;
Pasha-like he holds his place,
Hated, envied and admired.
How you gobble life, my friend;
Wine, and woman soft and pink!
Well, each tether has its end:
Sir, it's later than you think.

See yon living scarecrow pass
With a wild and wolfish stare
At each empty absinthe glass,
As if he saw Heaven there.
Poor damned wretch, to end your pain
There is still the Greater Drink.
Yonder waits the sanguine Seine . . .
It is later than you think.

Lastly, you who read; aye, you
Who this very line may scan:
Think of all you planned to do . . .
Have you done the best you can?
See! the tavern lights are low;
Black's the night, and how you shrink!
God! and is it time to go?
Ah! the clock is always slow;

It is later than you think;
Sadly later than you think;
Far, far later than you think.

THE ABSINTHE DRINKERS

He's yonder, on the terrace of the Café de la Paix,
The little wizened Spanish man, I see him every day.
He's sitting with his Pernod on his customary chair;
He's staring at the passers with his customary stare.
He never takes his piercing eyes from off that moving throng,
That current cosmopolitan meandering along:
Dark diplomats from Martinique, pale Rastas from Peru,
An Englishman from Bloomsbury, a Yank from Kalamazoo;
A poet from Montmartre's heights, a dapper little Jap,
Exotic citizens of all the countries on the map;

A tourist horde from every land that's underneath the sun—
That little wizened Spanish man, he misses never one.
Oh, foul or fair he's always there, and many a drink he buys,
And there's a fire of red desire within his hollow eyes.
And sipping of my Pernod, and a-knowing what I know,
Sometimes I want to shriek aloud and give away the show.
I've lost my nerve; he's haunting me; he's like a beast of prey,
That Spanish man that's watching at the Café de la Paix.

Say! Listen and I'll tell you all . . . the day was growing dim,
And I was with my Pernod at the table next to him;
And he was sitting soberly as if he were asleep,
When suddenly he seemed to tense, like tiger for a leap.
And then he swung around to me, his hand went to his hip,
My heart was beating like a gong—my arm was in his grip;
His eyes were glaring into mine; aye, though I shrank with fear,
His fetid breath was on my face, his voice was in my ear:

"Excuse my *brusquerie*," he hissed; "but, sir, do you suppose—
That portly man who passed us had a *wen upon his nose?*"

And then a last it dawned on me, the fellow must be mad;
And when I soothingly replied: "I do not think he had,"
The little wizened Spanish man subsided in his chair,
And shrouded in his raven cloak resumed his owlish stare.
But when I tried to slip away he turned and glared at me,
And oh, that fishlike face of his was sinister to see:
"Forgive me if I startled you; of course you think I'm queer;
No doubt you wonder who I am, so solitary here;
You question why the passers-by I piercingly review . . .
Well, listen, my bibacious friend, I'll tell my tale to you.

"It happened twenty years ago, and in another land:
A maiden young and beautiful, two suitors for her hand.
My rival was the lucky one; I vowed I would repay;
Revenge has mellowed in my heart, it's rotten ripe to-day.
My happy rival skipped away, vamoosed, he left no trace;
And so I'm waiting, waiting here to meet him face to face;
For has it not been ever said that all the world one day
Will pass in pilgrimage before the Café de la Paix?"

"But, sir," I made remonstrance, "if it's twenty years ago,
You'd scarcely recognize him now, he must have altered so."
The little wizened Spanish man he laughed a hideous laugh,
And from his cloak he quickly drew a faded photograph.
"You're right," said he, "but there are traits (oh, this you must
    allow)
That never change; Lopez was fat, he must be fatter now.
His paunch is senatorial, he cannot see his toes,
I'm sure of it; and then, behold! that wen upon his nose.
I'm looking for a man like that. I'll wait and wait until . . ."

"What will you do?" I sharply cried; he answered me: "Why,
    kill!
He robbed me of my happiness—nay, stranger, do not start;
I'll firmly and politely put—a bullet in his heart."

And then that little Spanish man, with big cigar alight,
Uprose and shook my trembling hand and vanished in the night.
And I went home and thought of him and had a dreadful dream
Of portly men with each a wen, and woke up with a scream.
And sure enough, next morning, as I prowled the Boulevard,
A portly man with wenny nose roamed into my regard;
Then like a flash I ran to him and clutched him by the arm:
"Oh, sir," said I, "I do not wish to see you come to harm;
But if your life you value aught, I beg, entreat and pray—
Don't pass before the terrace of the Café de la Paix."
That portly man he looked at me with such a startled air,
Then bolted like a rabbit down the rue Michaudière.
"Ha! ha! I've saved a life," I thought; and laughed in my relief,
And straightway joined the Spanish man o'er his *apéritif*.
And thus each day I dodged about and kept the strictest guard
For portly men with each a wen upon the Boulevard.
And then I hailed my Spanish pal, and sitting in the sun,
We ordered many Pernods and we drank them every one.
And sternly he would stare and stare until my hand would shake,
And grimly he would glare and glare until my heart would
    quake.
And I would say: "Alphonso, lad, I must expostulate;
Why keep alive for twenty years the furnace of your hate?
Perhaps his wedded life was hell; and you, at least, are free . . ."
"That's where you've got it wrong," he snarled; "the fool she
    took was *me*.
My rival sneaked, threw up the sponge, betrayed himself a churl:

'Twas he who got the happiness, I only got—the girl."
With that he looked so devil-like he made me creep and shrink,
And there was nothing else to do but buy another drink.

Now yonder like a blot of ink he sits across the way,
Upon the smiling terrace of the Café de la Paix;
That little wizened Spanish man, his face is ghastly white,
His eyes are staring, staring like a tiger's in the night.
I know within his evil heart the fires of hate are fanned,
I know his automatic's ready waiting to his hand.
I know a tragedy is near. I dread, I have no peace . . .
Oh, don't you think I ought to go and call upon the police?
Look there . . . he's rising up . . . my God! He leaps from out
    his place . . .
Yon millionaire from Argentine . . . the two are face to
    face . . .
A shot! A shriek! A heavy fall! A huddled heap! Oh, see
The little wizened Spanish man is dancing in his glee. . . .
I'm sick . . . I'm faint . . . I'm going mad. . . . Oh, please
    take me away . . .
There's BLOOD upon the terrace of the Café de la Paix. . . .

THE BOHEMIAN

Up in my garret bleak and bare
I tilted back on my broken chair,
And my three old pals were with me there,
          Hunger and Thirst and Cold;
Hunger scowled at his scurvy mate:
Cold cowered down by the hollow grate,
And I hated them with a deadly hate
          As old as life is old.

So up in my garret that's near the sky
I smiled a smile that was thin and dry:
"You've roomed with me twenty year," said I,
          "Hunger and Thirst and Cold;
But now, begone down the broken stair!
I've suffered enough of your spite . . . so there!"
Bang! Bang! I slapped on the table bare
          A glittering heap of gold.

"Red flames will jewel my wine to-night;
I'll loose my belt that you've lugged so tight;
Ha! Ha! Dame Fortune is smiling bright;
          The stuff of my brain I've sold;
Canaille of the gutter, up! Away!
You've battened on me for a bitter-long day;
But I'm driving you forth, and forever and aye,
          Hunger and Thirst and Cold."

So I kicked them out with a scornful roar;

Yet, oh, they turned at the garret door;
Quietly there they spoke once more:
    "The tale is not all told.
It's *au revoir*, but it's not good-by;
We're yours, old chap, till the day you die;
Laugh on, you fool! Oh, you'll never defy
    Hunger and Thirst and Cold."

THE JOY OF BEING POOR

I

Let others sing of gold and gear, the joy of being rich;
But oh, the days when I was poor, a vagrant in a ditch!
When every dawn was like a gem, so radiant and rare,
And I had but a single coat, and not a single care;
When I would feast right royally on bacon, bread and beer,
And dig into a stack of hay and doze like any peer;
When I would wash beside a brook my solitary shirt,
And though it dried upon my back I never took a hurt;
When I went romping down the road contemptuous of care,
And slapped Adventure on the back—by Gad! we were a pair;
When, though my pockets lacked a coin, and though my coat
  was old,
The largess of the stars was mine, and all the sunset gold;
When time was only made for fools, and free as air was I,
And hard I hit and hard I lived beneath the open sky;
When all the roads were one to me, and each had its allure . . .
Ye Gods! these were the happy days, the days when I was poor.

II

Or else, again, old pal of mine, do you recall the times
You struggled with your storyettes, I wrestled with my rhymes;
Oh, we were happy, were we not?—we used to live so "high"
(A little bit of broken roof between us and the sky);
Upon the forge of art we toiled with hammer and with tongs;
You told me all your ripping yarns, I sang to you my songs.

114

Our hats were frayed, our jackets patched, our boots were down
 at heel,
But oh, the happy men were we, although we lacked a meal.
And if I sold a bit of rhyme, or if you placed a tale,
What feasts we had of tenderloins and apple-tarts and ale!
And yet how often we would dine as cheerful as you please,
Beside our little friendly fire on coffee, bread and cheese.
We lived upon the ragged edge, and grub was never sure,
But oh, these were the happy days, the days when we were poor.

III

Alas! old man, we're wealthy now, it's sad beyond a doubt;
We cannot dodge prosperity, success has found us out.
Your eye is very dull and drear, my brow is creased with care,
We realize how hard it is to be a millionaire.
The burden's heavy on our backs—you're thinking of your
 rents,
I'm worrying if I'll invest in five or six per cents.
We've limousines, and marble halls, and flunkeys by the score,
We play the part . . . but say, old chap, oh, isn't it a bore?
We work like slaves, we eat too much, we put on evening dress;
We've everything a man can want, I think . . . but happiness.

Come, let us sneak away, old chum; forget that we are rich,
And earn an honest appetite, and scratch an honest itch.
Let's be two jolly garreteers, up seven flights of stairs,
And wear old clothes and just pretend we aren't millionaires;
And wonder how we'll pay the rent, and scribble ream on ream,
And sup on sausages and tea, and laugh and loaf and dream.

And when we're tired of that, my friend, oh, you will come with
 me;

And we will seek the sunlit roads that lie beside the sea.
We'll know the joy the gipsy knows, the freedom nothing mars,
The golden treasure-gates of dawn, the mintage of the stars.
We'll smoke our pipes and watch the pot, and feed the crackling
    fire,
And sing like two old jolly boys, and dance to heart's desire;
We'll climb the hill and ford the brook and camp upon the
    moor . . .
Old chap, let's haste, I'm mad to taste the Joy of Being Poor.

MY MASTERPIECE

It's slim and trim and bound in blue;
Its leaves are crisp and edged with gold;
Its words are simple, stalwart too;
Its thoughts are tender, wise and bold.
Its pages scintillate with wit;
Its pathos clutches at my throat:
Oh, how I love each line of it!
That Little Book I Never Wrote.

In dreams I see it praised and prized
By all, from plowman unto peer;
It's pencil-marked and memorized,
It's loaned (and not returned, I fear);
It's worn and torn and travel-tossed,
And even dusky natives quote
That classic that the world has lost,
The Little Book I Never Wrote.

Poor ghost! For homes you've failed to cheer,
For grieving hearts uncomforted,
Don't haunt me now. . . . Alas! I fear
The fire of Inspiration's dead.
A humdrum way I go to-night,
From all I hoped and dreamed remote:
Too late . . . a better man must write
That Little Book I Never Wrote.

THE OUTLAW

A WILD and woeful race he ran
Of lust and sin by land and sea;
Until, abhorred of God and man,
They swung him from the gallows-tree.
And then he climbed the Starry Stair,
And dumb and naked and alone,
With head unbowed and brazen glare,
He stood before the Judgment Throne.

The Keeper of the Records spoke:
"This man, O Lord, has mocked Thy Name.
The weak have wept beneath his yoke,
The strong have fled before his flame.
The blood of babes is on his sword;
His life is evil to the brim:
Look down, decree his doom, O Lord!
Lo! there is none will speak for him."

The golden trumpets blew a blast
That echoed in the crypts of Hell,
For there was Judgment to be passed,
And lips were hushed and silence fell.
The man was mute; he made no stir,
Erect before the Judgment Seat . . .
When all at once a mongrel cur
Crept out and cowered and licked his feet.

It licked his feet with whining cry.
Come Heav'n, come Hell, what did it care?
It leapt, it tried to catch his eye;
Its master, yea, its God was there.
Then, as a thrill of wonder sped
Through throngs of shining seraphim,
The Judge of All looked down and said:
"Lo! here is ONE who pleads for him.

"And who shall love of these the least,
And who by word or look or deed
Shall pity show to bird or beast,
By Me shall have a friend in need.
Aye, though his sin be black as night,
And though he stand 'mid men alone,
He shall be softened in My sight,
And find a pleader by My Throne.

"So let this man to glory win;
From life to life salvation glean;
By pain and sacrifice and sin,
Until he stand before Me—*clean*.
For he who loves the least of these
(And here I say and here repeat)
Shall win himself an angel's pleas
For Mercy at My Judgment Seat."

FINISTÈRE

Hurrah! I'm off to Finistère, to Finistère, to Finistère;
My satchel's swinging on my back, my staff is in my hand;
I've twenty *louis* in my purse, I know the sun and sea are there,
And so I'm starting out to-day to tramp the golden land.
I'll go alone and glorying, with on my lips a song of joy;
I'll leave behind the city with its canker and its care;
I'll swing along so sturdily—oh, won't I be the happy boy!
A-singing on the rocky roads, the roads of Finistère.

Oh, have you been to Finistère, and do you know a whin-grey
town
That echoes to the clatter of a thousand wooden shoes?
And have you seen the fisher-girls go gallivantin' up and down,
And watched the tawny boats go out, and heard the roaring
crews?
Oh, would you sit with pipe and bowl, and dream upon some
sunny quay,
Or would you walk the windy heath and drink the cooler air;
Oh, would you seek a cradled cove and tussle with the topaz
sea!—
Pack up your kit to-morrow, lad, and haste to Finistère.

Oh, I will go to Finistère, there's nothing that can hold me back.
I'll laugh with Yves and Léon, and I'll chaff with Rose and
Jeanne;
I'll seek the little, quaint *buvette* that's kept by Mother Mer-
drinac,
Who wears a cap of many frills, and swears just like a man.
I'll yarn with hearty, hairy chaps who dance and leap and crack
their heels;

Who swallow cupfuls of cognac and never turn a hair;
I'll watch the nut-brown boats come in with mullet, plaice and
    conger eels,
The jewelled harvest of the sea they reap in Finistère.

Yes, I'll come back from Finistère with memories of shining
    days,
Of scaly nets and salty men in overalls of brown;
Of ancient women knitting as they watch the tethered cattle
    graze
By little nestling beaches where the gorse goes blazing down;
Of headlands silvering the sea, of Calvarys against the sky,
Of scorn of angry sunsets, and of Carnac grim and bare;
Oh, won't I have the leaping veins, and tawny cheek and spar-
    kling eye,
When I come back to Montparnasse and dream of Finistère.

THE WONDERER

I WISH that I could understand
The moving marvel of my Hand;
I watch my fingers turn and twist,
The supple bending of my wrist,
The dainty touch of finger-tip,
The steel intensity of grip;
A tool of exquisite design,
With pride I think: "It's mine! It's mine!"

Then there's the wonder of my Eyes,
Where hills and houses, seas and skies,
In waves of light converge and pass,
And print themselves as on a glass.
Line, form and color live in me;
I am the Beauty that I see;
Ah! I could write a book of size
About the wonder of my Eyes.

What of the wonder of my Heart,
That plays so faithfully its part?
I hear it running sound and sweet;
It does not seem to miss a beat;
Between the cradle and the grave
It never falters, stanch and brave.
Alas! I wish I had the art
To tell the wonder of my Heart.

Then oh! but how can I explain
The wondrous wonder of my Brain?

That marvellous machine that brings
All consciousness of wonderings;
That lets me from myself leap out
And watch my body walk about;
It's hopeless—all my words are vain
To tell the wonder of my Brain.

But do not think, O patient friend,
Who reads these stanzas to the end,
That I myself would glorify. . . .
You're just as wonderful as I,
And all Creation in our view
Is quite as marvellous as you.
Come, let us on the sea-shore stand

And wonder at a grain of sand;
And then into the meadow pass
And marvel at a blade of grass;
Or cast our vision high and far
And thrill with wonder at a star;
A host of stars—night's holy tent
Huge-glittering with wonderment.

If wonder is in great and small,
Then what of Him who made it all?
In eyes and brain and heart and limb
Let's see the wondrous work of Him.
In house and hill and sward and sea,
In bird and beast and flower and tree,
In everything from sun to sod,
The wonder and the awe of God.

THE QUEST

I sought Him on the purple seas,
I sought Him on the peaks aflame;
Amid the gloom of giant trees
And canyons lone I called His name;
The wasted ways of earth I trod:
In vain! In vain! I found not God.

I sought Him in the hives of men,
The cities grand, the hamlets grey,
The temples old beyond my ken,
The tabernacles of to-day;
All life that is, from cloud to clod
I sought. . . . Alas! I found not God.

Then after roamings far and wide,
In streets and seas and deserts wild,
I came to stand at last beside
The death-bed of my little child.
Lo! as I bent beneath the rod
I raised my eyes . . . and there was God.

VICTORY STUFF

WHAT d'ye think, lad; what d'ye think,
As the roaring crowds go by?
As the banners flare and the brasses blare
And the great guns rend the sky?
As the women laugh like they'd all gone mad,
And the champagne glasses clink:
Oh, you're grippin' me hand so tightly, lad,
I'm a-wonderin': what d'ye think?

D'ye think o' the boys we used to know,
And how they'd have topped the fun?
Tom and Charlie, and Jack and Joe—
Gone now, every one.
How they'd have cheered as the joy-bells chime,
And they grabbed each girl for a kiss!
And now—they're rottin' in Flanders slime,
And they gave their lives—for *this*.

Or else d'ye think of the many a time
We wished we too was dead,
Up to our knees in the freezin' grime,
With the fires of hell overhead;
When the youth and the strength of us sapped away,
And we cursed in our rage and pain?
And yet—we haven't a word to say. . . .
We're glad. We'd do it again.

I'm scared that they pity us. Come, old boy,
Let's leave them their flags and their fuss.

We'd surely be hatin' to spoil their joy
With the sight of such wrecks as us.
Let's slip away quietly, you and me,
And we'll talk of our chums out there:
You with your eyes that'll never see,
Me that's wheeled in a chair.

GRANDAD

HEAVEN's mighty sweet, I guess;
Ain't no rush to git there;
Been a sinner, more or less;
Maybe wouldn't fit there.
Wicked still, bound to confess;
Might jest pine a bit there.

Heaven's swell, the preachers say:
Got so used to earth here;
Had such good times all the way,
Frolic, fun and mirth here;
Eighty Springs ago to-day,
Since I had my birth here.

Quite a spell of happy years.
Wish I could begin it;
Cloud and sunshine, laughter, tears,
Livin' every minute.
Women, too, the pretty dears;
Plenty of 'em in it.

Heaven! that's another tale.
Mightn't let me chew there.
Gotta have me pot of ale;
Would I like the brew there?
Maybe I'd get slack and stale—
No more chores to do there.

Here I weed the garden plot,
Scare the crows from pillage;

Simmer in the sun a lot,
Talk about the tillage.
Yarn of battles I have fought,
Greybeard of the village.

Heaven's mighty fine, I know. . . .
Still, it ain't so bad here.
See them maples all aglow;
Starlings seem so glad here:
I'll be mighty peeved to go,
Scrumptious times I've had here.

Lord, I know You'll understand.
With Your Light You'll lead me.
Though I'm not the pious brand,
I'm here when You need me.
 Gosh! I know that Heaven's GRAND,
But dang it! God, *don't speed me.*

THE BALLAD OF CASEY'S BILLY-GOAT

You've heard of "Casey at The Bat,"
And "Casey's Tabble Dote";
But now it's time
To write the rhyme
Of "Casey's Billy-goat."

Pat Casey had a billy-goat he gave the name of Shamus,
Because it was (the neighbours said) a national disgrace.
And sure enough that animal was eminently famous
For masticating every rag of laundry round the place.
From shirts to skirts prodigiously it proved its powers of chewing;
The question of digestion seemed to matter not at all;
But you'll agree, I think with me, its limit of misdoing
Was reached the day it swallowed Missis Rooney's ould red shawl.

Now Missis Annie Rooney was a winsome widow woman,
And many a bouncing boy had sought to make her change her name;
And living just across the way 'twas surely only human
A lonesome man like Casey should be wishfully the same.
So every Sunday, shaved and shined, he'd make the fine occasion
To call upon the lady, and she'd take his hat and coat;
And supping tea it seemed that she might yield to his persuasion,
But alas! he hadn't counted on that devastating goat.

For Shamus loved his master with a deep and dumb devotion,
And everywhere that Casey went that goat would want to go;

And though I cannot analyse a quadruped's emotion,
They said the baste was jealous, and I reckon it was so.
For every time that Casey went to call on Missis Rooney,
Beside the gate the goat would wait with woefulness intense;
Until one day it chanced that they were fast becoming spooney,
When Shamus spied that ould red shawl a-flutter on the fence.

Now Missis Rooney loved that shawl beyond all rhyme or
    reason,
And maybe 'twas an heirloom or a cherished souvenir;
For judging by the way she wore it season after season,
It might have been as precious as a product of Cashmere.
So Shamus strolled towards it, and no doubt the colour pleased
    him,
For he biffed it and he sniffed it, as most any goat might do;
Then his melancholy vanished as a sense of hunger seized him,
And he wagged his tail with rapture as he started in to chew

"Begorrah! you're a daisy," said the doting Mister Casey
To the blushing Widow Rooney as they parted at the door.
"Wid yer tinderness an' tazin' sure ye've set me heart a-blazin',
And I dread the day I'll nivver see me Annie anny more."
"Go on now wid yer blarney," said the widow softly sighing;
And she went to pull his whiskers, when dismay her bosom
    smote. . . .
Her ould red shawl! 'Twas missin' where she'd left it bravely
    drying—
Then she saw it disappearing—down the neck of Casey's goat.

Fiercely flamed her Irish temper. "Look!" says she, "the thavin'
    divvle!
Sure he's made me shawl his supper. Well, I hope it's to his taste;
But excuse me, Mister Casey, if I seem to be oncivil,

For I'll nivver wed a man wid such a misbegotten baste."
So she slammed the door and left him in a state of consternation,
And he couldn't understand it, till he saw that grinning goat;
Then with eloquence he cussed it, and his final fulmination
Was a poem of profanity impossible to quote.

So blasting goats and petticoats, and feeling downright sinful,
Despairfully he wandered in to Shinnigan's shebeen;
And straightway he proceeded to absorb a mighty skinful
Of the deadliest variety of Shinnigan's potheen.
And when he started homeward it was in the early morning,
But Shamus followed faithfully, a yard behind his back;
Then Casey slipped and stumbled, and without the slightest
        warning
Like a lump of lead he tumbled—right across the railway track.

And there he lay, serenely, and defied the powers to budge him,
Reposing like a baby, with his head upon a rail;
But Shamus seemed unhappy, and from time to time would
        nudge him,
Though his prods of protestation were without the least avail.
Then to that goatish mind, maybe, a sense of fell disaster
Came stealing like a spectre in the dim and dreary dawn;
For his bleat of warning blended with the snoring of his master
In a chorus of calamity—but Casey slumbered on.

Yet oh, that goat was troubled, for his efforts were redoubled;
Now he tugged at Casey's whisker, now he nibbled at his ear;
Now he shook him by the shoulder, and with fear becoming
        bolder,
He bellowed like a fog-horn, but the sleeper did not hear.
Then up and down the railway line he scampered for assistance;
But anxiously he hurried back and sought with tug and strain

To pull his master off the track . . . when sudden! in the distance
He heard the roar and rumble of the fast approaching train.

Did Shamus faint and falter? No, he stood there stark and splendid.
True, his tummy was distended, but he gave his horns a toss.
By them his goathood's honour would be gallantly defended,
And if their valour failed him—he would perish with his boss.
So dauntlessly he lowered his head, and ever clearer, clearer,
He heard the throb and thunder of the Continental Mail.
He would face that mighty monster. It was coming nearer, nearer;
He would fight it, he would smite it, but he'd never show his tail.

Can you see that hirsute hero, standing there in tragic glory?
Can you hear the Pullman porters shrieking horror to the sky?
No, you can't; because my story has no end so grim and gory,
For Shamus did not perish and his master did not die.
At this very present moment Casey swaggers hale and hearty,
And Shamus strolls beside him with a bright bell at his throat;
While the recent Missis Rooney is the gayest of the party,
For now she's Missis Casey and she's crazy for that goat.

You're wondering what happened? Well, you know that truth is stranger
Than the wildest brand of fiction, so I'll tell you without shame. . . .
There was Shamus and his master in the face of awful danger,
And the giant locomotive dashing down in smoke and flame. . . .
What power on earth could save them? Yet a golden inspiration
To gods and goats alike may come, so in that brutish brain

A thought was born—*the ould red shawl*. . . . Then rearing
  with elation,
Like lightning Shamus *threw it up*—AND FLAGGED AND STOPPED
  THE TRAIN.

MATERNITY

THERE once was a Square, such a square little Square,
And he loved a trim Triangle;
But she was a flirt and around her skirt
Vainly she made him dangle.
Oh he wanted to wed and he had no dread
Of domestic woes and wrangles;
For he thought that his fate was to procreate
Cute little Squares and Triangles.

Now it happened one day on that geometric way
There swaggered a big bold Cube,
With a haughty stare and he made that Square
Have the air of a perfect boob;
To his solid spell the Triangle fell,
And she thrilled with love's sweet sickness,
For she took delight in his breadth and height—
But how she adored his thickness!

So that poor little Square just died of despair,
For his love he could not strangle;
While the bold Cube led to the bridal bed
That cute and acute Triangle.
The Square's sad lot she has long forgot,
And his passionate pretensions . . .
For she dotes on her kids— Oh such cute *Pyramids*
In a world of three dimensions.

LAUGHTER

I LAUGH at Life: its antics make for me a giddy game,
Where only foolish fellows take themselves with solemn aim.
I laugh at pomp and vanity, at riches, rank and pride;
At social inanity, at swagger, swank and side.
At poets, pastry-cooks and kings, at folk sublime and small,
Who fuss about a thousand things that matter not at all;
At those who dream of name and fame, at those who scheme for
    pelf. . . .
But best of all the laughing game—is laughing at myself.

Some poet chap has labelled man the noblest work of God:
I see myself a charlatan, a humbug and a fraud.
Yea, 'spite of show and shallow wit, and sentimental drool,
I know myself a hypocrite, a coward and a fool.
And though I kick myself with glee profoundly on the pants,
I'm little worse, it seems to me, than other human ants.
For if you probe your private mind, impervious to shame,
Oh, Gentle Reader, you may find you're much about the same.

Then let us mock with ancient mirth this comic, cosmic plan;
The stars are laughing at the earth; God's greatest joke is man.
For laughter is a buckler bright, and scorn a shining spear;
So let us laugh with all our might at folly, fraud and fear.
Yet on our sorry selves be spent our most sardonic glee.
Oh don't pay life the compliment to take it *seriously*.
For he who can himself despise, be surgeon to the bone,
May win to worth in others' eyes, to wisdom in his own.

INSPIRATION

How often have I started out
With no thought in my noddle,
And wandered here and there about,
Where fancy bade me toddle;
Till feeling faunlike in my glee
I've voiced some gay distiches,
Returning joyfully to tea,
A poem in my britches.

A-squatting on a thymy slope
With vast of sky about me,
I've scribbled on an envelope
The rhymes the hills would shout me;
The couplets that the trees would call,
The lays the breezes proffered . . .
Oh no, I didn't *think* at all—
I took what Nature offered.

For that's the way you ought to write—
Without a trace of trouble;
Be super-charged with high delight
And let the words out-bubble;
Be voice of vale and wood and stream
Without design or proem:
Then rouse from out a golden dream
To find you've made a poem.

So I'll go forth with mind a blank,
And sea and sky will spell me;

And lolling on a thymy bank
I'll take down what they tell me;
As Mother Nature speaks to me
Her words I'll gaily docket,
So I'll come singing home to tea
A poem in my pocket.

THE BATTLE OF THE BULGE

This year an ocean trip I took, and as I am a Scot
And like to get my money's worth I never missed a
      meal.
In spite of Neptune's nastiness I ate an awful lot,
Yet felt as fit as if we sailed upon an even keel.
But now that I am home again I'm stricken with dis-
      gust;
How many pounds of fat I've gained I'd rather not
      divulge:
Well, anyway, I mean to take this tummy down or bust,
So here I'm suet-strafing in the
                        Battle of the Bulge.

No more will sausage, bacon, eggs provide my break-
      fast fare;
On lobster I will never lunch, with mounds of *mayon-
      naise*.
At tea I'll Spartanly eschew the chocolate *éclair;*
Roast duckling and *pêche melba* shall not consummate
      my days.
No more nocturnal ice-box raids, midnight spaghetti
      feeds;
On slabs of *pâté de foie gras* I vow I won't indulge:
Let bran and cottage cheese suffice my gastronomic
      needs,
And lettuce be my ally in the
                        Battle of the Bulge.

To hell with you, ignoble paunch, abhorrent in my
    sight!
I gaze at your rotundity, and savage is my frown.
I'll rub you and I'll scrub you and I'll drub you day
    and night,
But by the gods of symmetry I swear I'll get you down.
Your smooth and smug convexity, by heck! I will
    subdue,
And when you tucker in again with joy will l refulge;
No longer of my toes will you obstruct my downward
    view . . .
With might and main I'll fight to gain the
                   Battle of the Bulge.

YELLOW

One pearly day of early May
I strolled upon the sand,
And saw, say half-a-mile away,
A man with gun in hand;
A dog was cowering to his will,
As slow he sought to creep
Upon a dozen ducks so still
They seemed to be asleep.

When like a streak the dog dashed out,
The ducks flashed up in flight;
The fellow gave a savage shout
And cursed with all his might.
Then as I stood somewhat amazed
And gazed with eyes agog,
With bitter rage his gun he raised
And blazed and shot the dog.

You know how dogs can yelp with pain;
Its blood soaked in the sand,
And yet it crawled to him again
And tried to lick his hand.
"Forgive me, Lord, for what I've done,"
It seemed as if it said,
But once again he raised his gun:
This time he shot it—dead.

What could I do? What could I say?
'Twas such a lonely place.

Tongue-tied I saw him stride away,
I never saw his face.
I should have bawled the bastard out:
A yellow dog he slew;
But worse, he proved beyond a doubt
That—I was yellow too.

PANTHEIST

Lolling on a bank of thyme
Drunk with Spring I made this rhyme....

Though peoples perish in defeat,
And races suffer to survive,
The sunshine never was so sweet,
So vast the joy to be alive;
The laughing leaves, the glowing grass
Proclaim how good it is to be;
The pines are lyric as I pass,
The hills hosannas sing to me.

Pink roses ring yon placid palm,
Soft shines the blossom of the peach;
The sapphire sea is satin calm,
With bell-like tinkle on the beach;
A lizard lazes in the sun,
A bee is bumbling to my hand;
Shy breezes whisper: "You are one
With us because you understand."

Yea, I am one with all I see,
With wind and wave, with pine and palm;
Their very elements in me
Are fused to make me what I am.
Through me their common life-stream flows,
And when I yield this human breath,
In leaf and blossom, bud and rose,
Live on I will ... There is no Death.

Oh, let me flee from woeful things,
And listen to the linnet's song;
To solitude my spirit clings,
To sunny woodlands I belong.
O foolish men! Yourselves destroy,
But I from pain would win surcease. . . .
O Earth, grant me eternal joy!
O Nature—everlasting peace!

                    Amen.

HOBO

A father's pride I used to know,
A mother's love was mine;
For swinish husks I let them go,
And bedded with the swine.
Since then I've come on evil days
And most of life is hell;
But even swine have winsome ways
When once you know them well.

One time I guessed I'd cease to roam,
And greet the folks again;
And so I rode the rods to home
And through the window pane
I saw them weary, worn and grey . . .
I gazed from garden gloom,
And like sweet, shiny saints were they
In that sweet, shiny room.

D'ye think I hollered out: "Hullo!"
The prodigal to play,
And eat the fatted calf? Ah no,
I cursed and ran away.
My eyes were blears of whisky tears
As to a pub I ran:
But once at least I beat the beast
And proved myself a man.

Oh, some day I am going back,
But I'll have gold galore;

I'll wear a suit of sober black
And knock upon the door.
I'll tell them how I've made a stake,
We'll have the grandest time. . . .
"*Say, Mister, give a guy a break:*
For Crissake, spare a dime."

STAMP COLLECTOR

My worldly wealth I hoard in albums three,
My life collection of rare postage stamps;
My room is cold and bare as you can see,
My coat is old and shabby as a tramp's;
Yet more to me than balances in banks,
My albums three are worth a million francs.

I keep them in that box beside my bed,
For who would dream such treasures it could hold;
But every day I take them out and spread
Each page, to gloat like miser o'er his gold:
Dearer to me than could be child or wife,
I would defend them with my very life.

They *are* my very life, for every night
Over my catalogues I pore and pore;
I recognize rare items with delight,
Nothing I read but philatelic lore;
And when some specimen of choice I buy,
In all the world there's none more glad than I.

Behold my gem, my British penny black;
To pay its price I starved myself a year;
And many a night my dinner I would lack,
But when I bought it, oh, what radiant cheer!
Hitler made war that day—I did not care,
So long as my collection he would spare.

Look—my triangular Cape of Good Hope.
To purchase it I had to sell my car.

Now in my pocket for some *sous* I grope
To pay my omnibus when home is far,
And I am cold and hungry and footsore,
In haste to add some beauty to my store.

This very day, ah, what a joy was mine,
When in a dingy dealer's shop I found
This *franc* vermillion, eighteen forty-nine . . .
How painfully my heart began to pound!
(It's weak, they say) I paid the modest price
And tremblingly I vanished in a trice.

But oh, my dream is that some day of days,
I might discover a Mauritius blue,
Poking among the stamp-bins of the *quais*;
Who knows! They say there are but two;
Yet if a third one I should ever spy,
I think—God help me! I should faint and die. . . .

Poor Monsieur Pons, he's cold and dead,
One of those stamp-collecting cranks.
His garret held no crust of bread,
But albums worth a million francs.
On them his income he would spend,
By philatelic frenzy driven:
What did it profit in the end. . . .
You can't take stamps to Heaven.

SENTIMENTAL SHARK

Give me a cabin in the woods
Where not a human soul intrudes;
Where I can sit beside a stream
Beneath a balsam bough and dream,
And every morning see arise
The sun like bird of paradise;
Then go down to the creek and fish
A speckled trout for breakfast dish,
And fry it at an ember fire—
Ah! there's the life of my desire.

Alas! I'm tied to Wall Street where
They reckon me a millionaire,
And sometimes in a day alone
I gain a fortune o'er the 'phone.
Yet I to be a man was made,
And here I ply this sorry trade
Of Company manipulation,
Of selling short and stock inflation:
I whom God meant to rope a steer,
Fate made a Wall Street buccaneer.

Old Timer, how I envy you
Who do the things I long to do.
Oh, I would swap you all my riches
To step into your buckskin britches.
Your ragged shirt and rugged health
I'd take in trade for all my wealth.

Then shorn of fortune you would see
How drunk with freedom I would be;
I'd kick so hard, I'd kick so high,
I'd kick the moon clean from the sky.

Aye, gold to me is less than brass,
And jewels mean no more than glass.
My gold is sunshine and my gems
The glint of dew on grassy stems . . .
Yet though I hate my guts it's true
Time sorta makes you used to you;
And so I will not gripe too much
Because I have the Midas touch,
But doodle on my swivel chair,
Resigned to be a millionaire.

PULLMAN PORTER

The porter in the Pullman car
Was charming, as they sometimes are.
He scanned my baggage tags: "Are you
The man who wrote of Lady Lou?"
When I said "yes" he made a fuss—
Oh, he was most assiduous;
And I was pleased to think that he
Enjoyed my brand of poetry.

He was forever at my call,
So when we got to Montreal
And he had brushed me off, I said:
"I'm glad my poems you have read,
I feel quite flattered, I confess,
And if you give me your address
I'll send you (autographed, of course)
One of my little books of verse."

He smiled—his teeth were white as milk;
He spoke—his voice was soft as silk.
I recognized, despite his skin,
The perfect gentleman within.
Then courteously he made reply:
"I thank you kindly, Sir, but I
With many other cherished tome
Have all your books of verse at home.

"When I was quite a little boy
I used to savour them with joy;

And now my daughter, aged three,
Can tell the tale of Sam McGee;
While Tom, my son, that's only two,
Has heard the yarn of Dan McGrew. . . .
Don't think your stuff I'm not applaudin'—
My taste is Eliot and Auden."

So as we gravely bade adieu
I felt quite snubbed—and so would you.
And yet I shook him by the hand,
Impressed that he could understand
The works of those two tops I mention,
So far beyond *my* comprehension—
A humble bard of boys and barmen,
Disdained, alas! by Pullman carmen.

THE ORDINARY MAN

If you and I should chance to meet,
I guess you wouldn't care;
I'm sure you'd pass me in the street
As if I wasn't there;
You'd never look me in the face,
My modest mug to scan,
Because I'm just a commonplace
    And Ordinary Man.

But then, it may be, you are too
A guy of every day,
Who does the job he's told to do
And takes the wife his pay;
Who makes a home and kids his care,
And works with pick or pen. . . .
Why, Pal, I guess we're just a pair
    Of Ordinary Men.

We plug away and make no fuss,
Our feats are never crowned;
And yet it's common coves like us
Who make the world go round.
And as we steer a steady course
By God's predestined plan,
Hats off to that almighty Force:
    THE ORDINARY MAN.

YOUR POEM

My poem may be yours indeed
In melody and tone,
If in its rhythm you can read
A music of your own;
If in its pale woof you can weave
Your lovelier design,
'Twill make my lyric, I believe,
  More yours than mine.

I'm but a prompter at the best;
Crude cues are all I give.
In simple stanzas I suggest—
'Tis you who make them live.
My bit of rhyme is but a frame,
And if my lines you quote,
I think, although they bear my name,
  'Tis you who wrote.

Yours is the beauty that you see
In any words I sing;
The magic and the melody
'Tis you, dear friend, who bring.
Yea, by the glory and the gleam,
The loveliness that lures
Your thought to starry heights of dream,
  The poem's yours.

RIVIERA HONEYMOON

Beneath the trees I lounged at ease
And watched them speed the pace;
They swerved and swung, they clutched and clung,
They leapt in roaring chase;
The crowd was thrilled, a chap was killed:
It was a splendid race.

Two men, they say, went West that day,
But I knew only one;
Geranium-red his blood was spread
And blazoned in the sun;
A lightning crash . . . Lo! in a flash
His racing days were done.

I did not see—such sights to me
Appallingly are grim;
But for a girl of sunny curl
I would not mention him,
That English lad with grin so glad,
And racing togs so trim.

His motor bike was painted like
A postal box of red.
'Twas gay to view . . . "We bought it new,"
A voice beside me said.
"Our little bit we blew on it
The day that we were wed.

"We took a chance: through sunny France
We flashed with flaunting power.

With happy smiles a hundred miles
Or more we made an hour.
Like flame we hurled into a world
A-foam with fruit and flower.

"Our means were small; we risked them all
This famous race to win,
So we can take a shop and make
Our bread—one must begin.
We're not afraid; Jack has his trade:
He's bright as brassy pin.

"Hark! Here they come; uphill they hum;
My lad has second place;
They swing, they roar, they pass once more,
Now Jack sprints up the pace.
They're whizzing past . . . At last, at last
He leads—he'll *win* the race.

"Another round . . . They leap, they bound,
But—where O where is he?"
And then the girl with sunny curl
Turned chalk-faced unto me,
Within her eyes a wild surmise
It was not good to see.

They say like thunder-bolt he crashed
Into a wall of stone;
To bloody muck his face was mashed,
He died without a moan;
In borrowed black the girl went back
To London Town alone.

Beneath the trees I lounged at ease
And saw them pep the pace;

They swerved and swung, they clutched and clung,
And roaring was the chase:
Two men, they say, were croaked that day—
It was a glorious race.

AN OLIVE FIRE

An olive fire's a lovely thing;
Somehow it makes me think of Spring
As in my grate it over-spills
With dancing flames like daffodils.
They flirt and frolic, twist and twine,
The brassy fire-irons wink and shine. . . .
Leap gold, you flamelets! Laugh and sing:
An olive fire's a lovely thing.

An olive fire's a household shrine:
A crusty loaf, a jug of wine,
An apple and a chunk of cheese—
Oh I could be content with these.
But if my cruse of oil is there,
To fry a fresh-caught fish, I swear
I do not envy any king,
As sitting by my hearth I sing:
An olive fire's a lovely thing.

When old and worn, of life I tire,
I'll sit before an olive fire,
And watch the feather ash like snow
As softly as a rose heart glow;
The tawny roots will loose their hoard
Of sunbeams centuries have stored,
And flames like yellow chickens cheep,
Till in my heart Peace is so deep:
With hands prayer-clasped I sleep . . . and sleep.

TAKE IT EASY

When I was boxing in the ring
In 'Frisco back in ninety-seven,
I used to make five bucks a fling
To give as good as I was given.
But when I felt too fighting gay,
And tried to be a dinger-donger,
My second, Mike Muldoon, would say:
"Go easy, kid; you'll stay the longer."

When I was on the Yukon trail
The boys would warn, when things were bleakest,
The weakest link's the one to fail—
Said I: "By Gosh! I won't be weakest."
So I would strain with might and main,
Striving to prove I was the stronger,
Till Sourdough Sam would snap: "Goddam!
Go easy, son; you'll last the longer."

So all you lads of eighty odd
Take my advice—you'll never rue it:
Be quite prepared to meet your God,
But don't stampede yourselves to do it.
Just cultivate a sober gait;
Don't emulate the lively conger;
No need to race, slow down the pace,
Go easy, Pals—you'll linger longer.

COMPENSATION PETE

He used to say: "There ain't a doubt
Misfortune is a bitter pill,
But if you only pry it out
You'll find there's good in every ill.
There's comfort in the worst of woe,
There's consolation in defeat . . .
Oh what a solace-seeker! So
We called him Compensation Pete.

He lost his wealth—but was he pipped?
Why no—"That's fine," he used to say.
"I've got the government plumb gypped—
No more damn income tax to pay.
From cares of property set free,
And with no pesky social ties,
Why, even poverty may be
A benediction in disguise."

He lost his health: "Okay," he said;
"I'm getting on, may be it's best.
I've always loved to lie abed,
And now I have the *right* to rest.
Such heaps o' things I want to do,
I'll have no time to fret or brood.
I'll read the dam ol' Bible through:
Guess it'll do me plenty good."

He had that line of sunny shine
That makes a blessing of a curse,

And he would say: "Don't let's repine,
Though things are bad they might be worse."
And so he cherished to the end
Philosophy so sane and sweet
That everybody was his friend . . .
With optimism hard to beat—
God bless old Compensation Pete.

MAKING GOOD

No man can be a failure if he *thinks* he's a success;
He may not own his roof-tree overhead,
He may be on his uppers and have hocked his evening dress—
(Financially speaking—in the red.)
He may have chronic shortage to repay the old home mortgage,
And almost be a bankrupt in his biz.,
But though he skips his dinner,
And each day he's growing thinner,
If he thinks he is a winner,

Then he is.

But when I say Success I mean the sublimated kind;
A man may gain it yet be on the dole.
To me it's music of the heart and sunshine of the mind,
Serenity and sweetness of the soul.
You may not have a brace of bucks to jingle in your jeans,
Far less the dough to buy a motor car;
But though the row you're hoeing
May be grim, ungodly going,
If you think the skies are glowing—

Then they are.

For a poor man may be wealthy and a millionaire may fall,
It all depends upon the point of view.
It's the sterling of your spirit tips the balance of the scale,
It's optimism, and it's up to you.
For what I figure as success is simple Happiness,
The consummate contentment of your mood:

You may toil with brain and sinew,
And though little wealth it win you,
If there's health and hope within you—

You've made good.

BROTHER JIM

My brother Jim's a millionaire,
While I have scarce a penny;
His face is creased with lines of care,
While my mug hasn't any.
With inwardness his eyes are dim,
While mine laugh out in glee,
And though I ought to envy him,
I think he envies me.

He has a chateau, I a shack,
And humble I should be
To see his stately Cadillac
Beside my jalopy.
With chain of gold his belly's girt,
His beard is barber trim;
Yet bristle-chinned with ragged shirt,
I do not envy Jim.

My brother is a man of weight;
For every civic plum
He grabs within the pie of state,
While I am just a bum.
Last Winter he was near to croak
With gastric ulcers grim. . . .
Ah no! although I'm stony broke
I will not envy Jim.

He gets the work, I get the fun;
He has no time for play;

Whereas with paddle, rod and gun
My life's a holiday.
As over crabbed script he pores
I scan the sky's blue rim. . . .
Oh boy! While I have God's outdoors
I'll never envy Jim.

CONTENTMENT

An ancient gaffer once I knew,
Who puffed a pipe and tossed a tankard;
He claimed a hundred years and two,
And for a dozen more he hankered;
So o'er a pint I asked how he
Had kept his timbers tight together;
He grinned and answered: "It maun be
Because I likes all kinds o' weather.

"For every morn when I get up
I lights me clay pipe wi' a cinder,
And as me mug o' tea I sup
I looks from out the cottage winder;
And if it's shade or if it's shine
Or wind or snow befit to freeze me,
I always say: 'Well, now, that's fine . . .
It's just the sort o' day to please me.'

"For I have found it wise in life
To take the luck the way it's coming;
A wake, a worry or a wife—
Just carry on and keep a-humming.
And so I lights me pipe o' clay,
And though the morn on blizzard borders,
I chuckle in me guts and say:
'It's just the day the doctor orders.'"

A mighty good philosophy
Thought I, and leads to longer living,

To make the best of things that be,
And take the weather of God's giving;
So though the sky be ashen grey,
And winds be edged and sleet be slanting,
Heap faggots on the fire and say:
"It's just the kind of day I'm wanting."

SECURITY

Young man, gather gold and gear,
They will wear you well;
You can thumb your nose at fear,
Wish the horde in hell.
With the haughty you can be
Insolent and bold:
Young man, if you would be free,
Gather gear and gold.

Mellow man of middle age,
Buy a little farm;
Then let revolution rage,
You will take no harm.
Cold and hunger, hand in hand,
May red ruin spread;
With your little bit of land
You'll be warm and fed.

Old man, seek the smiling sun,
Wall yourself away;
Dream aloof from everyone
In a garden gay.
Let no grieving mar your mood,
Have no truck with tears;
Greet each day with gratitude—
Glean a hundred years.

ANT HILL

Black ants have made a musty mound
My purple pine tree under,
And I am often to be found,
Regarding it with wonder.
Yet as I watch, somehow it's odd,
Above their busy striving
I feel like an ironic god
Surveying human striving.

Then one day came my serving maid,
And just in time I caught her,
For on each lusty arm she weighed
A pail of boiling water.
Said she with glee: "When this I spill,
Of life they'll soon be lacking."
Said I: "If even one you kill,
You bitch! I'll send you packing."

Just think—ten thousand eager lives
In that toil-won upcasting,
Their homes, their babies and their wives
Destroyed in one fell blasting!
Imagine that swift-scalding hell! . . .
And though, mayhap, it seem a
Fantastic, far-fetched parallel
Remember . . . Hiroshima.

MY PINEY WOOD

I have a tiny piney wood;
My trees are only fifty,
Yet give me shade and solitude
For they are thick and thrifty.
And every day to me they fling
With largess undenying,
Fat cones to make my kettle sing
And keep my pan a-frying.

Go buy yourself a piney wood
If you have gold for spending,
Where you can dream in mellow mood
With peace and joy unending;
Where you can cheerfully retreat
Beyond all churchly chiding,
And make yourself a temple sweet
Of rapturous abiding.

Oh Silence has a secret voice
That claims the soul for portal,
And those who hear it may rejoice
Since they are more than mortal.
So sitting in my piney wood
When soft the owl is winging,
As still as Druid stone I brood . . .
For hark! the *stars* are singing.

GOD'S SKALLYWAGS

The God of Scribes looked down and saw
The bitter band of seven,
Who had outraged his holy law
And lost their hope of Heaven:
Came Villon, petty thief and pimp,
And obscene Baudelaire,
And Byron with his lecher limp,
And Poe with starry stare.

And Wilde who lived his hell on earth,
And Burns, the bawdy bard,
And Francis Thompson, from his birth
Malevolently starred. . . .
As like a line of livid ghosts
They stared to Paradise,
The galaxy of Heaven's hosts
Looked down in soft surmise.

Said God: "You bastards of my love,
You are my chosen sons;
Come, I will set you high above
These merely holy ones.
Your sins you've paid in gall and grief,
So to these radiant skies,
Seducer, drunkard, dopester, thief,
Immortally arise.

"I am your Father, fond and just,
And all your folly see;

Your bestiality and lust
I also know in me.
You did the task I gave to you . . .
Arise and sit beside
My Son, the best belovéd, who
Was also crucified."

THE UNDER-DOGS

What have we done, Oh Lord, that we
    Are evil starred?
How have we erred and sinned to be
    So scourged and scarred?
Lash us, Oh Lord, with scorpion whips,
    We can but run;
But harken to our piteous lips:
    What have we done?

How have we sinned to rouse your wrath,
    To earn your scorn?
Stony and steep has been our path
    Since we were born.
Oh for a sign, a hope, a word,
    A heaven glance;
Why is your hand against us, Lord?
    Give us a chance.

What shall we do, Oh God, to gain
    Your mercy seat?
Shall we live out our lives in pain
    And dark defeat?
Shall we in servitude bow low
    Unto the end?
How we would hope, could we but know
    You are our friend!

We are the disinherited,
    The doomed, the lost.

For breath, with dust and ashes fed,
              We pay the cost.
Dumb mouths! Yet though we bleed, with prayer
              We kiss the sword;
Aye, even dying we forbear
              To curse Thee, Lord.

TEA ON THE LAWN

It was foretold by sybils three
That in an air crash he would die.
"I'll fool their prophecy," said he;
"You won't get me to go on high.
Howe'er the need for haste and speed,
I'll never, never, never fly."

It's true he travelled everywhere,
Afar and near, by land and sea,
Yet he would never go by air
And chance an evil destiny.
Always by ship or rail he went—
For him no sky-plane accident.

Then one day walking on the heath
He watched a pilot chap on high,
And chuckled as he stood beneath
That lad a-looping in the sky.
Feeling so safe and full of glee
Serenely he went home to tea.

With buttered toast he told his wife:
"My dear, you can't say I've been rash;
Three fortune tellers said my life
Would end up in an air-plane crash.
But see! I'm here so safe and sound:
By gad! I'll never leave the ground.

"For me no baptism of air;
It's in my bed I mean to die.

Behold yon crazy fool up there,
A-cutting capers in the sky.
His motor makes a devilish ᐁin . . .
Look! Look! He's gone into a spin.

"He's dashing downward—*Oh my God!*" . . .
Alas! he never finished tea.
The motor ploughed the garden sod
And in the crash a corpse was he:
Proving that no man can frustrate
The merciless design of Fate.

REPENTANCE

"If you repent," the Parson said,
"Your sins will be forgiven.
Aye, even on your dying bed
You're not too late for Heaven."

That's just my cup of tea, I thought,
Though for my sins I sorrow;
Since salvation is easy bought
I will repent . . . to-morrow.

To-morrow and to-morrow went,
But though my youth was flying,
I was reluctant to repent,
Having no fear of dying.

'Tis plain, I mused, the more I sin,
(To Satan's jubilation)
When I repent the more I'll win
Celestial approbation.

So still I sin, and though I fail
To get snow-whitely shriven,
My timing's good: I hope to hail
The last bus up to Heaven.

ODETTE

Along the Seine with empty belly
I wandered in the sunny morn;
My legs were wobbly as a jelly,
I wished that I had ne'er been born.
Of hope, alas! I hadn't any,
And I was weak from want of food;
When one has not a bloody penny,
Why, even suicide seems good.

I stumbled, seeking not to show it;
The quay was lined with bins of books,
But though I once had been a poet,
I gave them bleak and bitter looks.
Then shrinking in a faded cover,
Reminding me from musty shelf
Of days when I was life's gay lover,
I saw—a book I wrote myself.

The dealer watched me with suspicion;
My boots were cracked, my coat was old.
Oh sure it was a first edition,
For not a copy had I sold.
I opened to its dedication:
"To my adorable Odette."
Then . . . then I stared with consternation:
The pages were unsevered yet.

Yet she inspired its finest numbers . . .
And then a memory awoke

From half a century of slumbers—
A note, a *mille* did I not poke
Within it . . . There! Who would believe it?
As crisp and clean it was today,
And so I hastened to retrieve it,
Put back the book and walk away.

They say bread cast upon the waters
Returneth after many days.
Odette was one of Joy's fair daughters,
Yet sadly fickle in her ways.
Now I've wherewith for bread and butter,
And yet somehow my spirit grieves,
As paying garret rent I mutter:
"The trollop didn't cut the leaves."

DUELLO

A Frenchman and an Englishman
Resolved to fight a duel,
And hit upon a savage plan,
Because their hate was cruel.
They each would fire a single shot
In room of darkness pitchy,
And who was killed or who was not
Would hang on fingers twitchy.

The room was bare and dark as death,
And each ferocious fighter
Could hear his fierce opponent's breath
And clutched his pistol tighter.
Then Gaston fired—the bullet hissed
On its destructive mission . . .
"Thank God!" said John Bull. "He has missed."
The Frenchman cried: "Perdition!"

Then silence followed like a spell,
And as the Briton sought to
Reply he wondered where the hell
His Gallic foe had got to.
And then he thought: "I'll mercy show,
Since Hades Is a dire place
To send a fellow to—and so
I'll blaze up through the fireplace."

So up the chimney he let fly,
Of grace a gallant henchman;

When lo! a sudden, sooty cry,
And down there crashed the Frenchman . . .
But if this yarn in France you tell,
Although its vein be skittish,
I think it might be just as well
To make your Frenchman—British.

MY FUTURE

"Let's make him a sailor," said Father,
"And he will adventure the sea."
"A soldier," said Mother, "is rather
What I would prefer him to be."
"A lawyer," said Father, "would please me,
For then he could draw up my will."
"A doctor," said Mother, "would ease me;
Maybe he could give me a pill."

Said Father: "Let's make him a curate,
A Bishop in gaiters to be."
Said Mother: "I couldn't endure it
To have Willie preaching to *me*."
Said Father: "Let him be a poet;
So often he's gathering wool."
Said Mother with temper: "Oh stow it!
You know it, a poet's a fool."

Said Father: "Your son is a duffer,
A stupid and mischievous elf."
Said Mother, who's rather a huffer:
"That's right—he takes after yourself."
Controlling parental emotion,
They turned to me, seeking a cue,
And sudden conceived the bright notion
To ask what I *wanted* to do.

Said I: "My ambition is modest:
A clown in a circus I'd be,

And turn somersaults in the sawdust
With audience laughing at me."
... Poor parents! they're dead and decaying,
But I am a clown, as you see;
And though in no circus I'm playing,
How people are laughing at me!

DYSPEPTIC CLERK

I think I'll buy a little field,
Though scant am I of pelf,
And hold the hope that it may yield
A living for myself;
For I have toiled ten thousand days
With ledger and with pen,
And I am sick of city ways
And soured with city men.

So I will plant my little plot
With lettuce, beans and peas;
Potatoes too—oh quite a lot,
And pear and apple trees.
My carrots will be coral pink,
My turnips ivory;
And I'll forget my pen and ink,
And office slavery.

My hut shall have a single room
Monastically bare;
A faggot fire for winter gloom,
A table and a chair.
A Frugalist I call myself,
My needs are oh so small;
My luxury a classic shelf
Of poets on the wall.

Here as I dream, how grey and cold
The City seems to me;

Another world of green and gold
Incessantly I see.
So I will fling my pen away,
And learn a hoe to wield:
A cashbook and a stool today . . .
Soon, soon a Little Field.

BRITANNICA

Sheer knowledge was the goal he sought;
He did not wed, and being thrifty,
A new *Britannica* he bought,
And settled down, though nearing fifty,
Its sturdy volumes twenty-four
To ponder o'er and o'er and o'er.

He started with the letter A,
And read with ardour undiminished,
Nor hesitated by the way
Until the letter Z he finished;
And though some subjects rather irked,
Not even the most dull he shirked.

So every year he made the trip
From A to Z and back returning;
He never once relaxed his grip
Although his midnight oil was burning;
Till grey professors straight from college
Would compliment him on his knowledge.

Yet he was happy all the while
Though little lucre he was earning,
And he would tell you with a smile:
"Life's truest treasure lies in learning.
What satisfaction it can bring
To know something of everything!"

And so he read and read and read
To slake his thirst for information;

But when they told me he was dead
How I was filled with consternation!
To think his store of learned lore
Was lost, alas! for evermore.

So his *Britannica* I bought,
Of knowledge to acquire a smatter.
Alas! it gathers dust a lot,
But I reflect—what does it matter?
On brain of scholar, sot and swine,
(On his replete, and arid mine)
With equal zest the worm doth dine.

MUGUET

'Twas on the sacred First of May
I made a sentimental sally
To buy myself a slender spray
Of pearly lily of the valley;
And setting it beside my bed,
Dream back the smile of one now dead.

But when I asked how much a spray?
The figure seemed so astronomic
I rather fear that my dismay
Must have appeared a little comic.
The price, the shopgirl gravely said,
Alas! was fifteen francs a head.

However, I said: "Give me three,
And wrap them in a silver paper,
And I will take them home with me,
And light an 'in memoriam' taper,
To one whose smile, so heaven bright,
Was wont to make my darkness light."

Then lo! I saw beside me stand
A woman shabby, old and grey,
Who pointed with a trembling hand
And shyly asked: "How much are they?"
But when I told her, sadly said:
"I'll save my francs for milk and bread.

"Yet I've a daughter just sixteen,
Long sick abed and oh so sad.

I thought—well, how they would have been
A gift, maybe, to make her glad . . ."
And then I saw her eyes caress
My blossoms with such wistfulness.

I gave them: sought my garret bare,
Knowing that she whom I had loved,
Although no blooms I brought her there,
Would have so tenderly approved . . .
And in the dark I lay awhile,
Seeing again her radiant smile.

THE WEDDING RING

I pawned my sick wife's wedding ring,
To drink and make myself a beast.
I got the most that it would bring,
Of golden coins the very least.
With stealth into her room I crept
And stole it from her as she slept.

I do not think that she will know,
As in its place I left a band
Of brass that has a brighter glow
And gleamed upon her withered hand.
I do not think that she can tell
The change—she does not see too well.

Pray God, she doesn't find me out.
I'd rather far I would be dead.
Yet yesterday she seemed to doubt,
And looking at me long she said:
"My finger must have shrunk, because
My ring seems bigger than it was."

She gazed at it so wistfully,
And one big tear rolled down her cheek.
Said she: "You'll bury it with me . . ."
I was so moved I could not speak.
Oh wretched me! How whisky can
Bring out the devil in a man!

And yet I know she loves me still,
As on the morn that we were wed;

And darkly guess I also will
Be doomed the day shat she is dead.
And yet I swear, before she's gone,
I will retrieve her ring from pawn.

I'll get it though I have to steal,
Then when to ease her bitter pain
They give her sleep oh I will feel
Her hand and slip it on again;
Through tears her wasted face I'll see,
And pray to God: "Oh pity me!"

THE HAT

In city shop a hat I saw
That so my fancy seemed to strike,
I gave my wage to buy the straw,
And make myself a one the like.

I wore it to the village fair;
Oh proud I was, though poor was I.
The maids looked at me with a stare,
The lads looked at me with a sigh.

I wore it Sunday to the Mass.
The other girls wore handkerchiefs.
I saw them darkly watch and pass,
With sullen smiles, with hidden griefs.

And then with sobbing fear I fled,
But they waylayed me on the street,
And tore the hat from off my head,
And trampled it beneath their feet.

I sought the Church; my grief was wild,
And by my mother's grave I sat:
... I've never cried for clay-cold child,
As I wept for that ruined hat.

NORMANDY PEASANT

They've taken all my fields of corn
   To make them strips of strife;
They've razed the house where I was born
   And lived in all my life.
Where once I jolted with content
   Along deep rutted lanes,
They've straddled runways of cement
   To ground their aeroplanes.

They've made me sell my bit of land
   And paid me with their gold.
Alas, they could not understand
   It was my heart I sold.
From my beloved soil bereft
   It was my soul I gave,
And now I know there's nothing left
   Between me and the grave.

They say that progress must go on
   Though darkly glooms the Pit.
Ah well, my life is nearly gone
   And I am glad of it.
Then buy my land and millions spend
   To sponsor war's red woe,
And what will be the awful end
   Thank God! I'll never know.

For oh the world is in a mess,
   And day by day grows worse;

I've had my bid of happiness
   And now I know the Curse
Of monstrous might and speed that's blind,
   And see, as fails my breath,
The doom of martyred humankind,
   When Science mates with Death.

I BELIEVE

It's my belief that every man
   Should do his share of work,
And in our economic plan
   No citizen should shirk.
That in return each one should get
   His meed of fold and food,
And feel that all his toil and sweat
   Is for the common good.

It's my belief that every chap
   Should have an equal start,
And there should be no handicap
   To hinder his depart;
That there be fairness in the fight,
   And justice in the race,
And every lad should have the right
   To win his proper place.

It's my belief that people should
   Be neither rich nor poor;
That none should suffer servitude,
   And all should be secure.
That wealth is loot, and rank is rot,
   And foul is class and clan;
That to succeed a man may not
   Exploit his brother man.

It's my belief that heritage
   And usury are wrong;

That each should win a worthy wage
  And sing an honest song. . . .
Not one like this—for though I rue
  The wrong of life, I flout it.
Alas! I'm not prepared to do
  A goddam thing about it.

RESENTMENT

A man's a mug to slog away
   And stint himself of ease,
When bureaucrats take half his pay
   To glut their treasuries.
A guy's a dope to work like hell
   To make one dollar two,
When most of it will go to swell
   The fiscal revenue.

So you who gripe at super-tax
   Of sixty-five per cent,
Why don't you blissfully relax,
   And beat the government?
Cut down to half the work you do,
   Contrive on less to live:
Go easy on the job and you
   Will have less gain to give.

Just plumb refuse to slave and sweat;
   Forbear to do your best,
When only half your wage you get
   And taxes claim the rest.
Although your talents go to rust,
   Your usefulness abate. . . .
Why make an extra dollar just
   To give it to the State?

If I possessed a million I
   Would change it all to gold,

And in a safe my bedside nigh
  My treasure I would hold.
And though a tenth each year I spent,
  I'd live in leisure lax
On capital—Oh! So content
  To bilk the income tax!

MODERATION

What pious people label vice
    I reckon mainly pleasure;
I deem that women, wine and dice
    Are good in modest measure;
Though sanctity and truth receive
    My hearty approbation,
Of all the virtues, I believe
    The best is Moderation.

Be moderate in love and hate,
    Soft pedal on emotion;
And never let your passion get
    The better of your caution.
Should Right or Leftist seek to goad
    You from the course that's level,
Stick to the middle of the road
    And send them to the devil.

Though rich the feast be moderate
    In eating and in drinking;
An appetite insatiate
    Is evil to my thinking.
Though ladies languidly await
    Your kisses, on your way shun
Their wiles, but—well, be moderate
    Even in moderation.

Avoid extremes: be moderate
    In saving and in spending;

An equable and easy gait
   Will win an easy ending. . . .
So here's to him of open mind,
   Of sense and toleration,
That hope of headlong human-kind,
   The Man of Moderation.

THE BRUISER

So iron-grim and icy cool
I bored in on him like a bull.
As if one with the solid ground
I took his blows round after round:
Glutton for punishment am I,
Rather than quit prepared to die.

Like dancing master was the boy,
Graceful and light, a boxer's joy.
He flapped a left and tapped a right—
I laughed because his blows were light;
The gong was like a golden chime,
As darkly I abode my time.

It's hard to stand ten grilling rounds.
I saw despite his leaps and bounds
That he was tired and failing fast;
But little longer could he last,
While I as solid as a rock
Grinned and withstood shock after shock.

Round eight: I launched to the attack.
I gave him all, held nothing back,
Disdained defence, with hammer blows:
The blood was spouting from his nose;
One eye, cut open, glistened wild . . .
Sudden he seemed a helpless child.

Round nine: They'd washed the blood away,
But bang! It spouted bright and gay.

His face was all a gory mask,
And yet no mercy would he ask.
Ah yes, the boy was gallant game,
Yet I must down him all the same.

Round ten: His eye like oyster gleamed.
I could have blinded him, it seemed.
Then as he weaved, faint and forlorn,
Strange pity in my heart was born.
I dropped my hands unto my side:
"For God's sake, strike me, lad!" I cried.

He struck me twice, two loving taps,
As if he understood, perhaps.
Then as the gong went like a knell,
Fainting into my arms he fell.
We kissed each other, he and I . . .
"*A draw!*" I heard the umpire cry.

NATURE MAN

The happiest man I ever knew
   Was scarcely clad at all;
He had no bath like me and you,
   But owned a waterfall.
And every sunrise he would wade
   The streamlet silver bright,
To stand beneath the clear cascade
          With sheer delight.

The happiest man I ever knew
   Lived in a forest glade;
His hut of palm-leaf and bamboo
   With his own hands he made.
And for his breakfast he would pick
   A bread-fruit from the tree,
Or lobster he would gaily flick
          From out the sea.

The happiest man I ever knew
   Could barely read or write,
But beer from honey he could brew
   To get drunk every night.
He had no wife as I'm aware,
   Nor any bastard brat,
But lived a life without a care,
          With laughter fat.

The happiest man I ever knew
   Was innocent of rent;

Low labour he would scorn to do
  And never owned a cent.
But he would strum an old guitar
  And sing a sultry song,
Insouciant as children are
            Of right and wrong.

The happiest man I ever knew
  Recked not of government;
His wants were simple and so few
  His life was pure content.
And as I thole this rancid mart,
  In which I plot and plan,
How glad I'd be, with all my heart,
            That happy man.

MONGREL

A puppy dog without a collar
  Annexed me on my evening walk;
His coat suggested fleas and squalor,
  His tail had never known a dock.
So humble, trusting, wistful was he,
  I gave his head a cautious pat,
Then I regretted it because he
  Accompanied me to my door-mat.

And there with morning milk I found him,
  Where he had slumbered all the night;
I could not with displeasure hound him,
  So wonderful was his delight.
And so with him I shared my porridge—
  Oh! How voraciously he ate!
And then I had the woeful courage
  To thrust him through the garden gate.

But there all morning long he waited;
  I had to sneak out by the back.
To hurt his feelings how I hated,
  Yet somehow he got on my track.
For down the road he sudden saw me
  And though in trees I tried to hide,
How pantingly he sought to paw me,
  And yelped with rapture by my side.

Poor dirty dog! I should have coshed him,
  But after all 'twas not his fault;

And so I took him home and washed him,
  —I'm that soft-hearted kind of dolt.
But then he looked so sadly thinner,
  Though speckless clean and airy bright,
I had to buck him up with dinner
  And keep him for another night.

And now he is a household fixture
  And never wants to leave my side;
A doggy dog, a mongrel mixture,
  I couldn't lose him if I tried.
His tail undocked is one wild wiggle,
  His heaven is my happy nod;
His life is one ecstatic wriggle,
  And I'm his God.

DIRT

Dirt is just matter out of place,
 So scientists aver;
But when I see a miner's face
 I wonder if they err.
For grit and grime and grease may be
 In God's constructive plan,
A symbol of nobility,
 The measure of a man.

There's nought so clean as honest dirt,
 So of its worth I sing;
I value more an oily shirt
 Than garment of a king.
There's nought so proud as honest sweat,
 And though its stink we cuss,
We kid-glove chaps are in the debt
 Of those who sweat for us.

It's dirt and sweat that makes us folks
 Proud as we are today;
We owe our wealth to weary blokes
 Befouled by soot and clay.
And where you see a belly fat
 A dozen more are lean. . . .
By God! I'd sooner doff my hat
 To washer-wife than queen.

So here's a song to dirt and sweat,
 A grace to grit and grime;

A hail to workers who beget
    The wonders of our time.
And as they gaze, though gutter-girt,
    To palaces enskied,
Let them believe, by sweat and dirt,
    They, too, are glorified.

MY HIGHLAND HOME

My mother spun the household wool,
  And all our kiddy clothes would make;
I used to go barefoot to school,
  While bannock took the place of cake.
One shirt a week was all I had,
  Our home was just a but-and-ben;
But oh I was the proudful lad,
  And life was rich with promise then.

Although I supped on milk and brose,
  And went to bed by candle-light,
I pored on books of noble prose,
  And longed like Bobbie Burns to write.
Now in this age of the machine
  I look back three-score years and ten:
With life so simple, sane and clean,
  Oh were we not more happy then?

We deemed not of electric light,
  Nor ever thought that we would fly;
Our sons were not called up to fight,
  And in a foreign field to die.
So now when threats of war appal,
  And millions cower to monster men,
Friends, don't you think that, after all,
  We were a heap more happy then?

THE BUTCHER

They say that ruthless Robespierre,
   That "sea-green incorruptible,"
To whom the nobs of nobles were
   By guillotines deductible,—
With necks of dukes at his demand
   Could peel an orange with one hand.

I've tried to do only twice,
   But though the oranges were Sèville,
I made a mush that wasn't nice,
   And damned old Robbie to the devil:
Well, in the end he went, by heck!
   For he, too, got it in the neck.

Aye, finally he lost his nob:
   ('Twas his pet "Maiden" did the chopping)
—I'm glad that was the last of Rob,
   But though the work he did was "topping,"
His triumph was, I understand,
   To peel an orange with one hand.

DARK PINE

If my life-force, by death decree,
Could find green haven in a tree,
And there in peace untroubled years
Could dream, immune from toil and tears,
Though I'm a lover of all trees
I would not favour one of these . . .

I would not choose a brittle palm
Beside a sea of senile calm;
Or willow droopily adream
Above bright babble of a stream.
No cypress would inhibit me
With dark and dour austerity;
Nor olive, shattering the light,
Nor poplar, purple in the night.
The sanctuary of my search
Would not be oak, nor ash, nor birch:
Ah no! Their comfort I decline,—
Let my life-force pervade a Pine.

Aye, when my soul shall sally forth
Let it be to the naked North,
And in a lone pine desolate
Achieve its fit and final fate;
A pine by arctic tempest torn,
Snow-scourged, wind-savaged and forlorn;
A viking trunk, a warrior tree,
A hostage to dark destiny

Of iron earth and icy sky,
That valiantly disdains to die.

There is the home where I would bide,
If trees like men had souls inside,—
Which is, of course, a fantasy
None could conceive but dolts like me . . .
Let others vision Heaven's gate,
Dark Pine, I dream for me you wait.

DAUNTLESS QUEST

Why seek to scale Mount Everest,
    Queen of the air?
Why strive to crown that cruel crest
    And deathward dare?
Said Mallory of dauntless quest:
    "Because it's there."

Why yearn with passion and with pain
    To storm the sky?
Why suffer,—sullen goals to gain,
    And fear defy?
" 'Tis not for glory or for gain
    We darkly die."

Why join the reckless, roving crew
    Of trail and tent?
Why grimly take the roads of rue,
    To doom hell-bent?
"Columbus, Cook and Cabot knew,
    And yet they went."

Why bid the woolly world goodbye
    To follow far,
Adventures under evil sky
    And sullen star?
Let men like Mallory reply:
    "Because they are."

INDEX TO FIRST LINES